BIG GROWTH
IMPACT

5.7

SECRETS to

GROW your business

GET more freedom &

GIVE back

MIKE SKRYPNEK

Book Cover, Inner Design and Layout by Andrea Leljak
Editing by Brianne Graham

Published by Fit Family Inc. Publishing: fitnetworks@shaw.ca

ISBN-13:978-1502327659
ISBN-10:1502327651

For information about permissions or about discounts for bulk orders or to book an event with the author or his colleagues or any other matter, please write to info@mikeskrypnek.com.

Disclaimer:
This book contains the opinions and ideas of the author and is offered for information purposes only.

The author and publisher specifically disclaim responsibility for any liability loss or risk personal or otherwise, which is incurred as a consequence, directly or indirectly, of the use and application of any of the contents of this book.

What others are saying about Mike Skrypnek:

"If you're ready to grow your business while making a positive difference, then read and absorb the strategies in this brilliant book by my friend Mike Skrypnek."

— JAMES MALINCHAK, Featured on ABC's Hit TV Show, *Secret Millionaire*. Founder, www.bigmoneyspeaker. com

---

What others have said about Big GROWTH Big IMPACT:

"Mike Skrypnek has put together a collection and blue print of unforgettable business as well as life lessons, easy to use strategies and principles that are invaluable to any business or entrepreneur. Mike will take you and your business on an easy-reader ride and magical journey to achieve the success you want now! I am recommending this book as a must read for all of my clients. Well done!"

— JOHN FORMICA, "Ex-Disney Guy" and America's Customer Experience Coach

---

"For me, success has always started with the GIVE. Mike's 57 secrets connected with the personal side of growing business, getting more freedom and giving back."

— JILL LUBLIN, 3X's Best Selling author and international speaker. Publicitycrashcourse.com/freegift

---

"Throughout this book Mike does an amazing job of leading you to clarity in all the facets of being a highly successful entrepreneur, as well as having a highly successful life."

— DIANNA CAMPBELL-SMITH, Registered Psychologist, Founder of Transform Counselling and Coaching

---

"Every page of 'Big Growth, Big Impact' reminds me of the first time I met Mike Skrypnek: he care about you and your overall success in all areas of your life. Let Mike show you how he has benefitted so many of his clients, friends and family using his simple formula to success:

GROW BIZ. GET FREEDOM. GIVE BACK.

"That simple philosophy fills the pages of this quick, impactful read."

— DR. DANNY BRASSELL, www.dannybrassell.com "America's Leading Reading Ambassador", Bestselling Author & Highly-Acclaimed Leadership Success Speaker

---

About Mike

Mike is an accomplished author and recognized as Canada's leading authority and speaker on connecting business and personal success with legacy giving. He has delivered motivating presentations for entrepreneurs, lawyers, financial planners, charities and the millionaire businessperson next door. Speaking to audiences of 20 to 200 people, Mike has entertained and inspired over 1,400 people in just the past two years. Through his guidance, he has helped re-direct over $2.2 million to charitable causes since 2012 and he has a lot more to do.

Mike's quick learning style and innovative marketing ideas have helped him create and dominate a niche financial advisory business focusing on serving the non-profit industry. He has been able to share his  insights and knowledge of sales and marketing to lead others to gain top of mind positioning with their prospective customers and grow their own unique business. Mike can teach anyone how to manage their time and their talent better to get more freedom to enjoy their lives and their family. He knows life without passion and purpose is a life wasted and he has been showing others how they can give back for big impact through their business and personally.

SPECIAL GIFT FOR YOU

To help you GROW your business, GET more freedom and GIVE back, I've put together additional free bonus resources for you at:

www.BigGROWTHBigIMPACTSummit.com
Enter code: BGBIFREEBONUS

Just enter the code and we'll give you access to:

- Free video interviews with Mike sharing secrets to implement your GROW marketing strategy, executing your GET freedom for you strategy, and the step by step directions on taking your own GIVE back action.

- Free video interview with one of North America's elite business and philanthropic leaders.

Go to
www.BigGROWTHBigIMPACTSummit.com
and enter code in my Live Chat box:

BGBIFREEBONUS

Help others GROW, GET and GIVE!

Share this book!

Retail: $19.95

Special Quantity Discounts

5 – 20 books	$17.95
21 – 50 books	$15.95
100 – 499 books	$14.95
500 + books	$10.95

To place an order, contact:

(403) 870-6775

info@mikeskrypnek.com

www.mikeskrypnek.com

www.BigGROWTHBigIMPACTSummit.com

CONTENTS

GROW your Business

GET MORE FREEDOM

GIVE BACK

INTRODUCTION

For the past twenty years, I have been working with entrepreneurs, visionaries, deal makers, philanthropists, and the "millionaires next door". I have raised millions for start-up companies and big ideas, guided families to legacy planning, and in the last couple years have helped direct over two million dollars to charitable causes. Naturally, I have made my share of mistakes, learned from them, made new ones, and learned from them as well. Along the way I have become wiser and more focused. During the last few years, I have been able to carve out a dominant position in an area of the investment management industry that my peers have often steered clear of. As a result, customers, friends, and associates have sought me out for my input and advice regularly, in hopes that I might be able to share strategic insights into what I know and what I have learned about business building for entrepreneurs growing their own niche businesses. This book is a formal way for me to share my wisdom and knowledge in an effort to help those visionaries.

My life turned on a dime in 2001 when my daughter Madison was born. Prior to that major life event, everything I had done — every business venture and every success and mistake — was made without much forethought, guidance or planning. I would say I paid considerably large "tuition" fees for the life experience gained when things went wrong. When Madison arrived on the scene, however, I promised myself, and my wife Sherri, that I would never again be surprised by my future successes.

I made a commitment to become an expert in investment

management. To do that, I needed to go back to school to learn my craft. At that time, it meant focusing on the academia and learning the science of investing from some of the most noted minds of the modern times, some Nobel laureates, and other innovative economists. In just a few years and a ton of hard work, I became extensively knowledgeable on managing wealth and investing high net worth clients' assets. I had always considered myself a life-long learner, but I hadn't done much of a job of it in the 1990s. I made up for lost time in a big way in the 2000s, and by the market crash in 2008 I was prepared to take my business to the next level ... even if it meant a re-start.

In 2009, I launched myself into the next phase of my investment and business career that has now become a key part of the foundation for the rest of my life. In less than four years, I worked harder than anyone around me and learned more in a short period of time than most of my peers. I had to because, almost a year into a global stock market collapse, I left two business partners and changed firms while risking significant loss of my client assets as well as the largest single endowment customer I had ever worked with. North America was reaching the final stages of the worst recession in over seventy years — only the "Great Depression" was worse. When the dust settled on my transition and during the height of investor fear and paranoia, I had only managed to move one fifth of my client assets with me — losing a $29 million endowment account and another $30 million in client assets to the appalling predatory behaviors of my previous partners. As 2010 began, I was starting over at 39 years old. I was looking forward, energized and excited about the future.

It is has now been over four years since the realization that I had only a fraction of my investment business and customers to build on. Since then, I have restored my business and have grown my revenue exponentially. Today, I feel as though I am just getting started. This is the third book that I have written in four years. I have become the dominant provider of tax and estate planning events for charities and their donors in Calgary. All the while I have been building the foundation for my future entrepreneur coaching business with a goal to help entrepreneurs give $100 million back to their communities in the next ten years. There is a *lot* of work to do.

So what was the most important change for me? Well, I embraced my passion for philanthropy and giving back and combined that with my expertise in guiding charities and donors to connect and uncover their legacy goals. I went through five years — and counting — of intense personal and business coaching. I researched and wrote white papers, many articles, and my first book — investing over $120,000 in this "educational process" thus far. My second book, *"Big Impact Giving"* was published simultaneously with this book, my third. I have been speaking to audiences across North America for the last three years — reaching nearly two thousand lawyers, accountants, financial advisers and planners, charity professionals, and high net worth families. My specialty is unique. I chose to focus on the non-profit industry niche. This is the area my peer group, many of them from the Gordon Gekko *"greed is good"* credo, call the NO-PROFIT industry. It has uniquely positioned me as Canada's leading authority on legacy planning and charitable giving. It has set the stage for a very lucrative investment advisory career and opened the window of opportunity for so much more in my life.

As the years have passed, clients, friends and entrepreneurs have sought me out for advice. They want to learn how I was able to dominate a highly specialized niche market and become successful doing so, and how my approach might work for them in their own unique business. They have looked to me for financial advice in some cases, but most were looking for strategic guidance in business decisions and opportunities. In response, I have evolved to a career path upon which strategic thinking is the core. Strategic thinking about wealth, about business, and about giving back has become the resource for which I have deep understanding and proven success.

This book was written to share the biggest tips I have learned and witnessed from the most successful entrepreneurs I have met, some of whom are now friends for whom I have a great deal of respect. In my first book *"Philanthropy; An Inspired Process"*, I ended with my One for One Million Challenge. That was my personal goal to help re-direct over one million dollars to charity every year for the rest of my life. In the past two years, I have exceeded that pace and have helped families re-direct over $2.2 million to charitable causes, while saving almost $1.1 million in income and estate taxes. Now, it seems as though my sights were short and my goal was low. In 2014, I decided to re-think my One for One Million goal and set the bar exponentially higher. My new goal was to help re-direct over **one hundred million** dollars to charitable causes over the next ten years. One of my early realizations was that guiding and planning for the *millionaire next door* wasn't going to get me there alone. It was a great start to big impact, but I was looking for greater leverage. The opportunity, I saw, was in the creative minds and exciting potential of entrepreneurs. I created Big GROWTH Big IMPACT to help teach entrepreneurs how to GROW their unique businesses large and very quickly, how to help them GET more freedom to enjoy their lives and their families, and how they can GIVE back to their community, the causes and institutions they care for most. This book, speaking, and my Big GROWTH Big IMPACT entrepreneur coaching business enables others to have an incredible impact. I urge you to read on, to learn, and to join me as we enjoy Big GROWTH and Big IMPACT. You can find out so much more and get started by registering for your first experience with me at www.biggrowthbigimpactsummit.com.

GROW your business

20 tips

to

faster and

bigger business growth

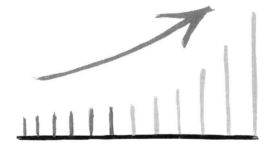

In the summer of 2014 I polled a few thousand entrepreneurs and asked them to share their biggest concerns and the area they'd like to learn better. The overwhelming number one response was that they all wanted to learn how to attract more customers to grow sales and make more money. They'd be willing to pay to learn how and spend time face-to-face in a seminar to do so. As such, I thought it best to start with the first and most important thing for entrepreneurs. That is, to grow their business bigger and faster — through more sales. To do this I have included twenty secret "tips" on sales and marketing you or your business that I have learned in my own experience, or from some of the most successful entrepreneurs.

SECRET TIP 1

> " know
>   who you are and
>   why you are doing
>   what you do "

———•———

What do you stand for? What are the principles that you have formed your life around? We learn these from our family, our life experiences and the environment we grow up in. Our philosophical belief systems form the foundation for what is important to us. Understanding what this means to us individually is important in shaping our connections with staff, stakeholders, and customers. The *"why"* runs a bit deeper. Our *"why"* is a connection between our principles — our personal and philosophical values — and our vision for the future. Jim Rohn once said, that "Philosophy drives attitude ... attitude drives action ... action drives results ... results drives lifestyle".

While the process of getting to who you are and expressing it in a public manner can be a bit challenging and even uncomfortable, you'll be surprised at how liberating it is to be YOU professionally and personally.

It will be okay to show people who you are and why you are passionate about what you do.

For me, it took a long time to build up the courage to share my desire to help others give and work philanthropically...while in the investment business. For most of my investment career, my peer group were largely from the "greed is good" way of thinking and having a heart was a bit too touchy-feely. So, I suppressed my desires to do more...until the markets crashed and it became clear there *had* to be something bigger and more important for people, and that I could help. My dedication to charity was an intentional step that my colleagues generally stayed away from. They viewed entering the non-profit field as the "no-profit" business. Well, it took me four or five years and I basically started from scratch. I started with a simple goal and I wrote it in the last chapter of my first book *"to help re-direct one million dollars per year to charity for the rest of my life"*. I built a business around connecting charities with the donors who love them and have just recorded nearly $1 million in gross sales over the past year. The bigger highlight of this growth in my business, in just over two years, was exceeding $2.1 million in facilitated charitable giving and over $1 million in income and estate taxes saved for my customers. Beyond my own business growth, the impact that will be realized for those I coach and guide, with that $2 million — and counting — of giving, will be immeasurable. It was done with a heart, helping others. Something I take great pride in.

WHAT EXPERIENCES HAVE SHAPED YOUR LIFE?

WHO ARE YOU?

WHY ARE YOU DOING WHAT YOU DO?

SECRET TIP 2

" know what you do
& keep it to yourself! "

This is your professional skill set; it is what you offer of benefit to your potential customers in your chosen field of business or in the marketplace. Do you serve and guide? Or do you lead through your products? Do you support and assist in the products or services you provide or do you create them? Having a clear understanding of what it is you've been trained to do, or have trained yourself to do is important. There are certain skills you have that others may not and your future customers will want.

People want to work with a company or person they trust, that they perceive to have their best interest at heart, and who are competent. When you are hired as the authority or expert, you are expected to have the skills needed to carry out the task. You must always understand that

your customers want you to know what you're doing, but they often do not care to hear the intricate details about it. They are most interested in **their** experience as a customer.

Keep this in mind before you spend time explaining how great you are...and what you have accomplished in your academic life. You should be more mindful of what your customers want.

What I "*do*" has two parts. The first and most important is my unique ability — personal connections, probing conversations to uncover true goals and values, and developing practical solutions to achieve those goals. The second is my professional skill set. I manage investment portfolios, guide customers on investing, cash flow, retirement funding, estate planning, charitable giving and planning, tax strategy, and strategic will planning. My skills support the implementation of appropriate tactics identified in our planning process. But let me tell you, the last thing most people want me to detail in our discussions is how smart I am at this, how the science of our investment tools works, and why the portfolio theory or factor models we use to make our decisions is better than other options in the marketplace. They want to hear about themselves, their own problems, and gain confidence that what I can do for them will get them closer to their goals.

What have you've been trained for?

What do you do?

What do your customers hope you do for them?

GROW your business

SECRET TIP 3

" be the authority

and

build your credibility "

Stand atop your mountain — become credible in the eyes of your customers. Authority positioning is a blend of experience, expertise, and perception. Your expertise allows you to position yourself in a market where your experience can be leveraged by customers who perceive you to be the most credible authority on the subject. There are so many ways that building credibility has been described by business coaches and marketing gurus. From climbing a credibility ladder to likening it to stairs, or mastery levels, it all really ends in the same place — the very top. I refer to it as "scaling the peak of a mountain". It is like climbing Mount Everest. So many people have now done it, yet, quite literally, billions of people have not. When someone says they've climbed Everest, we still are in awe at the achievement. In fact, that adventurer becomes instantly credible for somehow more than just the physical act of climbing the mountain. If someone reputable or a celebrity introduces this mountaineer, their credibility rises even higher.

Reaching the top of the mountain in a marketing sense is extremely challenging. From speaking, to writing articles, to being interviewed or endorsed by an expert or celebrity, there are many ways to begin the climb to credibility. However, in spite of thousands of books being published every year, writing a book creates instant credibility and places the author at the very peak of the mountain immediately.

The accomplishment of having written and published a book presents you as a perceived authority on a topic.

It is something so many people want to do and hope to, but writing, finishing, and publishing a book eludes the vast majority of those folks. Even in the simple accomplishment, people are impressed. Oprah took this acknowledgement to a whole new level and redefined how a celebrity endorsement of a book written by you will place you on the highest peak as the recognized authority.

I won't lie, while it sounds very simple, it can be extremely difficult to write a book. I found that simply putting words on paper was not too challenging ... and even organizing thoughts and ideas wasn't that difficult either, but knowing when it was done and being able to finish a book was the real trick. How many times have you heard someone say they have been working on a book...but never see it completed? Harder than writing a book, is finishing one. It doesn't have to be an epic, or the century's greatest novel. It just has to be a complete, sensible and topical book. My business coach, James Malinchak, when asked about some of his "smaller" books, responds to the typical critic by saying, *"the tiny little book I wrote is a heck of a lot better than the book you didn't"*.

The other thing about authors is that they have had to do the research to write the book, and thus they have become an authority on a particular subject. When it is a published work, people recognize and respect this. Finally, a book is content. Content is in huge demand. Quality, helpful content is invaluable. An author makes themselves a valuable resource for others who seek to learn more on a subject, or market one.

Early on, when I was working to establish myself as a credible authority by introducing my skill set and my thoughts on why a charity or endowment needed to work with such a smart guy as myself, I got nowhere. I couldn't get speaking opportunities; I didn't get any board meetings, and rarely even got an audience with the executive director. So, I wrote a white paper on the biggest challenges of the time faced by my target clients (charities and their endowments struggling to attract funding during a recession). Then, I wrote a book on philanthropy and the journey taken by donors moving from involved giving to committed philanthropy. It became the most meaningful "business card" I had ever possessed. Almost instantly, I gained credibility. I was invited to speak at numerous industry events and conferences. I was interviewed on the radio, in magazines. I was able to invite executive directors of charities to meet me in my office! I also received numerous opportunities to present to the board of directors of organizations I wanted to work with. Getting their ten minutes was always elusive before. Writing a book seemed magical. And it is. It is because it is hard. Everyone, if you ask them, seems to "have a book in them", but people rarely get it out. There is respect for the effort and an understanding that you've done the difficult work to become the authority. The only more credible endeavor would be to write two or more books … and have televised celebrity endorsement of your book. Remember the book you write is exponentially more powerful than the one your competitors won't write.

WHAT WILL YOU WRITE YOUR BOOK ABOUT?

WHAT DATE WILL YOU START WRITING?

WHAT DATE WILL YOU PUBLISH IT?

- ▶ YEAR:

- ▶ MONTH:

- ▶ DAY:

SECRET TIP 4

> " define your
> ideal customer
> & write it down! "

How can you serve anyone, sell anything or make any money if you don't know who your customer is? This is your perfect fit, or right fit customer. They are your match for millions of dollars. You will make more money, have less stress, and enjoy your work more when you work with the right customer. This is a detailed **written description** of whom you are selling your products, goods, or services to.

When writing your description, include their demographics, their gender, likes/dislikes, fears, concerns, greatest challenges, buying habits, values, and aspirations.

Identify those who are your current ideal customers and simply replicate them in your written description.

Then publish it! Identify how many of them there are, what they are trying to achieve, and how you can help them. Interview your current customers and write, in their words, what they value about your services or products. Share this information with all prospects in your marketing.

Here is the description of my ideal customer for my Strategic Financial Advisory business:

> *They are a married/common-law couple, or a single (divorced or widowed) female, who are 55-70 years old. They have been reasonably good savers, and have over one million dollars in invested assets, mostly in their registered investment plans. They own their homes with no mortgage and likely have*

a recreational property or other private investment asset. They are transitioning from their working years to their retirement years. Specifically, the shift is from having to work, to working or recreating by choice. They are the "millionaire next door" who are rather unassuming and know the value of a dollar. They respect expertise and are open to new ways of thinking. They are typically very intelligent and have been quite successful in their work or own business. They have had previous advisors who provided limited services with no planning process. They are not entirely displeased with their situation, yet know they need to do much more to plan for their future. Lastly, they are connected to the world and feel a strong desire to leave a legacy to their heirs and the causes and institutions which are important to them. They want to give charitably, but don't how to get there from where they are today.

Is your ideal customer description clear?

Describe your Ideal Customer

What is their demographic?

- Age
- Gender
- Geographic location
- Married or single
- List their personal traits or values

What stage of life are they in?

- Student
- Young working adult
- Married with young children
- Family with teens or university aged kids
- Empty nesters
- Accumulators
- Transition to retirement
- Retired

SECRET TIP 5

" know your
marketplace,
competitors and
landscape "

Learning the landscape you and your competitors share. This will help you understand the psyche of your customer. With this knowledge, you can better position yourself or your business as their desired solution.

Your current and future customers know what your competitors are doing and expect you to be at least the same as everyone else, but **hope** you'll be different — better.

Understanding your competition opens up doors to highlighting your unique offering. It is possible to deliver the same productive thing in a much better way. The hotel industry is fundamentally the same. It is focused on the provision of sleeping accommodation for travellers and tourists. However, it is really about the experience and expectations of your guests. If you compared the average accommodation of hotels ranging from the Best Western and Motel Six with the Four Seasons, you would see that in their simplest form all provide you with the standard bed, bathroom, and living space. In its most basic principle this is true, but anyone who has ever stayed at either extreme will tell you without a doubt that there is a gaping chasm between the Motel Six and Four Seasons. From the beds, to the linens, to the surroundings and location, to the details of bath products, and to housekeeping and service, everything is different. As basic as the requirements of your average traveller, the differences are monumental. Travelling and staying at the Motel Six is utilitarian and cost effective, while staying at the Four Seasons is a delightful experience and almost a destination in itself.

Learn from the success of others. Embracing the successful peers in your marketplace will help you learn from them and accept their unique offerings.

Once you are able to establish what "normal" is in your industry it is easy to take action to rise above your competitors. Think of coffee and coffee shops. Over thirty years ago, coffee in America was something that you paid a quarter for from a donut shop or cafeteria en route to wherever you were headed. The norm was cheap, no fuss, and utilitarian. When Starbucks launched and began a break-neck expansion in the late '80s and 1990s, they took the normal coffee shop and turned it into the "third place". Their stores became community focal points — social hubs. They sold coffee and specialty drinks that cost anywhere from $1 to $6 per cup! They smashed the norms and set the new standard. Some say they were "disruptive", but they really just differentiated their offering, with an emphasis on "place" and enjoyment of coffee as a beverage to be savored. They knew their market, understood their competitors, and set out to build their own standard for how their ideal customer would enjoy a simple cup of coffee.

"To stay vigorous, a company needs to provide a stimulating and challenging environment for all these types: the dreamer, the entrepreneur, the professional manager, and the leader. If it doesn't, it risks becoming yet another mediocre corporation."

— Howard Schultz, *Pour Your Heart Into It: How Starbucks Built a Company One Cup at a Time*

What are your competitors doing?

What does the customer expect?

What will you do differently and better?

SECRET TIP 6

" *position yourself*

with

credible partners "

Who influences your customers? Who will give you access to them? Who will endorse you? Those are three important questions that will guide you to your credibility partner. You must learn how you can *serve* the organizations, or people, which will provide you with a credible endorsement. Your input must *help* this partner achieve their goals. If you can help them serve their customers or stakeholders, they will allow you to work with them in their efforts to improve their customer relationships while tacitly endorsing your authority in a marketplace.

These are the centers of influence you look for who serve and guide your ideal customer. By positioning yourself as credible through such an endorsement, you become perceived as a useful or helpful resource recommended by someone they trust and respect.

How do people make decisions to buy or to use a service? They research. Where do they look? Today, they look to the internet and from the input of other people who comment or have experienced something. This is where we all hone our buying decisions. Your customers will be influenced by the overwhelming facts, the "cool factor" or by the ratings. They might look to the "likes" or views of others they respect or want to be respected by. If they don't know you, how will they trust you? In a commoditized industry, there might be a hundred (or thousands) services or products like yours — offering similar things. The endorsement of you as an authority or respected supplier by a source your customer respects or is connected to is powerful. It becomes a differentiator. If you were to walk up to someone who you thought might be a good customer at a social event and introduced yourself, the person might be hesitant to even speak to you or acknowledge you in a professional context. Even if you were to get past hello, convincing them you were someone they might want to work with can be a difficult task. They might even agree with everything you say and need your services....and still not become a customer. If you were to re-start at the beginning and obtain an introduction from one of their personal friends or a respected colleague as a credible resource, they might immediately be inclined to hear you out, and if they agree with your perspective or like your products, they will more than likely move toward becoming a customer. If they recognize you as an authority who a celebrity might have publicly endorsed, then they might even approach you BEFORE you get to them!

> The power of partnering with credible and trusted authorities will place you top of mind with potential customers.

In my legacy planning business, following a proprietary process called the Donor Motivation Program™, created by my coach, Scott Keffer, I partner with charities and serve them and their donors by providing helpful tax and estate planning information to protect their assets, and possibly leave more to charitable causes. We give them simple solutions to complex needs. We give them planned giving in a box. Charities want to be able to have more meaningful conversations with their donors about planned giving, but often do not have the resources or expertise to initiate the discussion consistently based on what is most important to the donor. That is their financial situation and concerns over succession and taxes. My target customer is the donor who is contemplating their own financial circumstances as they worry about having the income they need, protecting their financial assets from taxes and other threats, passing on their wealth to their heirs, and maybe charity. I serve the charity by helping them connect with their donors predictably and regularly. In turn, the charity endorses me as the authority on legacy planning to their donors. The charity gets a credible resource to educate their donors and inspire conversations, the donors learn something useful about taxes and estate planning, and I benefit from the marketing credibility positioning and possible introductions to ideal customers. It is a win-win-win ... oh yeah, and the ultimate outcome is when there is a charitable gift made and the beneficiaries of the charity are impacted. This adds a fourth "win" to the equation.

So stop asking for referrals from your current customers. They don't know how to sell you and while they might like you and respect you, they might not want to sell you to others. Identify, engage, and serve your future credibility partners. You will gain more leverage and build better relationships with future customers and you will remove the added dynamic of referrals from your customer relationships.

WHO INFLUENCES YOUR TARGET IDEAL CUSTOMERS?

WHO DO YOUR IDEAL CUSTOMERS TRUST OR LOOK UP TO?

How can you serve your credibility partner?

SECRET TIP 7

" always
be
marketing "

My business coach, James Malinchak, is always asked how he can get so many people to attend his business seminars or workshops and boot camps. His college speaking events are extremely well attended also, and he sells books, programs and courses at an amazing pace. Naturally, people want to know the absolute single best way he knows to get five hundred sure sales of customers through his events by marketing. He always says, "I don't know one best way to get five hundred sales, but I sure know fifty ways to get ten sales — and I do all of them!"

There are no miracle cures you can find, or magic pills. There is no mystical way to get big results. Everything requires effort and planning. It is just that the people who get the biggest results work smarter and harder than others to produce those results. They also quickly learn what works and what doesn't. Then, they focus their effort and energy on what does. James would tell you he didn't know fifty ways when he first started out, but he learned a new way (or more) every time he set out to sell a book or a course, a speaking gig, a tape, a CD, or whatever. By increasing the methods by which you market, you increase your chances of making sales. It is so simple, but generally people are lazy and stick to that one thing, hoping they will get results — so that they won't have to do all the other things! By using multiple methods, techniques, and approaches to marketing, you will find that you are also always marketing. This is because all communications, actions, conversations, and materials don't happen by accident or randomly, they were planned and designed to move uninterested people to become interested, then to engage them as prospects and ultimately as customers. Some methods are blunt instruments and others are surgically specific. You must use all of them in a defined process to build predictability, repeatability, and reliability to your sales efforts. Once used, you gain intelligence on their effectiveness and make adjustments, then repeat.

In hockey the goal is to score more times than your opponent. In order to score...you need to SHOOT the puck! Besides the score and the time remaining in the game, the most important statistic that is posted on all time clocks is the "shots on goal". More shots = more chances to score. This is the same with marketing. The more impressions, touches, asks, and conversations — the more sales. My motto on marketing is, "You don't ask, you don't get". Most people know that I have a passion for coaching in business, legacy planning, and sports. As "Coach Mike" I have been coaching my daughter's soccer teams for the past eight years. Most seasons have been winning affairs, with the exception of our most recent season. It was a bit of a challenge, to say the least. In fact, in the last 10 games of the season, our girls scored just twice! Repeatedly I was asked, what is wrong with the team? Why aren't they scoring? My simple response was — they were scoring as much as they were shooting, and that was not much. The girls asked how to fix this. I told them, simply, shoot more. So how do you shoot more? Well you practice getting opportunities to shoot and then shooting. You rehearse over and over until it is something you do instinctively, so in a game, nothing happens by accident. The ball is moved from the defence to the midfield and to the attacking forwards, they demand the ball, and then a shot is made at the net. The same applies to sales and marketing. If you never market, and never ask for the business, you will never sell anything.

Now if I taught the girls to pass, dribble or shoot using poor technique, would they have much luck repeating a successful shot? Not likely. If you use the wrong marketing techniques to sell, you will also have limited success. It is not enough to practice, but you need to apply the right techniques. Then you need to set up a measurable process and repeat. Sales should rarely happen accidently ... only accidents happen by accident.

When you have a message worth sharing and the ultimate effect of your efforts is to add value, make an impact, and enrich the lives of others, it is okay to market yourself and your business in any way possible to ensure you share your message with those who will benefit.

Marketing is not something you do to other people; it is something you do FOR them.

LIST 5 WAYS YOU ARE MARKETING TODAY

Name 10 more ways you could market your services or products?

SECRET TIP 8

" make

everything

a campaign "

Every marketing effort you make should revolve around some form of campaign. No matter how big or small. How do you effectively invite someone to an event? You could simply send an invitation and hope for the best. If you send enough, you will likely get someone to show up. This can be costly and provide extremely varied results in terms of who ends up attending.

One of my mastermind partners, who was in the investment real estate industry, was on the "hot seat" with six of us at the table. He asked us how he could get the best possible traffic to his new website that offered simple online courses for learning how to invest in real estate. Around the table, there were some incredible ideas and some great input from a couple experts on the topic of social media and building web traffic. One thing he had mentioned was that he had a network of two thousand affiliate realtors across the USA who marketed and promoted his program — for referrals. If you're paying attention to my message, you won't be surprised to learn that I suggested that he build an email campaign for his affiliate realtors to help them learn how to educate their own prospects such that they would be better and more receptive customers for their future offerings. In turn they would eventually drive traffic to the website that was established to give more investor education. He would provide a "realtor affiliate code" to identify which realtor referred their clients to the new site — in order to compensate them in the future if a fee was due. I estimated each of his 2,000 affiliate realtors could have as many as 1,000 prospects on their lists. If that was so, there was the potential that up to 2 million visitors could be directed to the website.

Naturally only a fraction will search for it, and less actually read anything on it, but that campaign would give positive, educational information directing and notifying two million qualified prospects that the website and his program existed. The key was that he built a campaign that his realtors would find useful, and would be able to execute simply.

You could also approach this using what I learned as one of the biggest selling lessons. It is the most effective sales method ever. It is NOT a brochure, or a poster or a website that I have created. It is the effective use of many types of sales material and endorsements interwoven into a marketing campaign that is designed to educate future potential customers why and how they can buy products or services from me.

EVERY marketing effort is a campaign.

I use what I call the "Campaign Cycle". This is a repeatable, predictable, and logical sequence of marketing messages that drive a customer to a decision whether to buy you or not. It is also used to filter out those who are not a good fit, and attract those who are seeking you. Through a simple, multiple message process using a variety of mediums (from email, to blogging, to direct mail, phone calls, and in-person) that serves to inform, educate, highlight concerns, inform, offer solutions, inform, make an offer, inform, make an offer again, close, follow up ... and repeat.

Try this approach, next time you are trying to build an audience for an event.

Inform: this could be a "save the date" notice or announcement. It is not a formal invitation.

Educate: this communication will remind your target audience what the landscape is for the particular message you are trying to convey. You can use a special report, or simply note that "*studies have shown*" ... or "*we interviewed 20 professionals in this market and this is what we found ...*"

Highlight Concerns: this communication will shine a light on the futility of your target prospects' current path of action. It will uncover their pain for their own discovery.

Inform: this is your solution to the prospects' greatest pain.

Offer (can be combined with above "inform"): this is your formal invitation along with the pricing and commitment required by the attendee.

Close: ACT NOW! Incentive to move fast and be first to register, to buy, or to pay.

Follow Up: confirm attendance or purchase decision before event/sale. Follow up again afterward to reduce or head off any sense of "buyer's remorse".

> ## TRY BUILDING YOUR OWN CAMPAIGN
> ## BY FILLING IN THE STEPS:

▶ WHAT IS YOUR SALE OR "EVENT"?

▶ WHEN IS IT?

▶ EDUCATE:

▶ INFORM:

▶ HIGHLIGHT CONCERNS:

▶ **INFORM:**

▶ **OFFER:**

▶ **CLOSE:**

▶ **FOLLOW UP:**

SECRET TIP 9

" help

your

customers

"

Become a serving leader in all you do. Leading is not confined to your staff and people around you; it also includes a responsibility to your customers. To be helpful to your customer it will require that you understand them. It is critical that you

learn what they need, what they like, and how you can help ease their pain or fulfill their desires to be better.

Become the trusted advisor or source for them by guiding in their self-discovery. Teach them how you will be able to help them. Making a commitment to serving your customer will position you closer to them.

When you solve their biggest challenges, offer what they want, or give them what they need, you move from a commodity to a resource. When you help your customer achieve their goals they become connected to you in a personal way. You become more than a supplier or advisor, but a trusted necessity. It is the same for personal services as it is for consumer products.

When Apple introduced the iPhone and iPod they made utilitarian technology (a phone and a music device) really cool. People want to be cool and feel cool. But they also **need** usability. While Apple brought cool, they also delivered intelligent and practical. Their products were simple and easy to use. People perceived more and paid more because they valued the offering. Apple helped a generation move deeper into connectivity. They re-inspired music, they changed social media and brought people together...in a cool way.

Serving your customer is also critical in a professional service role. For example, if you're a financial advisor, you serve by helping to ease pain. People WANT to be secure, feel confident about their finances and their future. People NEED a plan and tools to make that happen. You have a moral responsibility to use your knowledge, skills, and expertise to define goals for them based on their vision of the future and to deliver all they need to accomplish those goals.

WHAT DO YOUR CUSTOMERS WANT?

WHAT DO YOUR CUSTOMERS NEED?

HOW CAN YOU SERVE THEM?

SECRET TIP 10

" *provide*

process driven

solutions

"

Once you understand what your clients want and what they will need, you must identify the best possible solutions for them. This requires that you develop the skill to listen and learn. You are an expert, behave like one. Experts use their knowledge and experience to connect the dots and provide intelligent solutions. These are solutions to implement that result from a strategic planning process.

Every process starts with a clear vision for an ideal future outcome.

You use the ideal to build clarity and identify specific goals. Finally, the best solutions are uncovered to achieve those goals. This is the strategic approach. Such a process driven approach ends up identifying the best tactics. Seek out the best tactics and deliver them.

W. Edward Deming, an American engineer instrumental in inspiring the powerful Japanese post-war economic industrial recovery, famously stated that "if a person can't explain what they're doing as a process, they don't know what they're doing."

When marketing, your process should start with uncovering the "pain" being experienced by your customer and the ideal vision they have for their own future. In this effort, you will be able to create strategies to alleviate their challenges, while connecting their present with their future. The outputs of a strategic process will identify solutions (tactics) that are right for them. These solutions are the product of a strategic process. Revealing the futility of their current path and the most common experience, and then offering them a real, customized, and attainable solution that will remove their pain and connect them with their goals is helpful. Using processes to get there provides comfort. Having a process in place, that is describable in simple terms delineates your behavior and clarifies the approach you take to make decisions. Customers find this particularly reassuring. The biggest challenge for us is listening and observing what the customer is really saying, in order to start drawing the road map for them. It is the same for how we might think of our financial goals.

When we review our own goals, we might not be happy with the way things are now, but are afraid that we, or even someone else, might do something in ignorance to put us at greater risk. We also know what we hope the future could look like for us — our "Norman Rockwell" painting. The biggest problem is, because we're not experts in what it is that we're tackling, we have no idea how to get to our ideal, from where we are today. The authority who listens to us and uses an explainable process that gives us a clear strategic map to reach our goals will give us comfort. Because we are assured, we will gladly pay even more for their services. In order to ensure this, they must understand what we like and don't like. They must understand our biggest fears or concerns, and we must believe they see our vision for the future almost as well as we do.

List strategic steps you take
when moving a customer through your process

- ► DISCOVERY

- ► GOAL SETTING

- ► STRATEGIC PLANNING

- ► TACTIC IDENTIFICATION

- ► IMPLEMENTATION

- ► REVIEW

- ► IMPROVEMENTS

SECRET TIP 11

" *focus*

on your

unique ability "

Kathy Kolbe, renowned for her work in what is called "conative" skills identification and measurement, launched a rating system, called the Kolbe A Index which provides a rating of the Four Action Modes® she identified that represent human instincts used in creative problem solving. The premise is simple.

If you hope to get the most of people, place them in situations and careers where their strongest attributes are used.

Their natural behavioral tendencies will likely provide them more engagement, more possibilities for success, and greater passion for their activities.

The Strategic Coach™ program's first step for all new members is to have them take their Kolbe A Index test. This gives everyone an excellent idea of what they should be focusing on to begin their coaching experience. In fact, all coaching members walk around with name tags that have their Kolbe scores noted right on them. Behavioral testing focuses a person on what The Strategic Coach™ labelled the concept of "Unique Ability".

There are so many methods of testing your personality and behaviours, ranging from the Myers Briggs test, to Tom Rath's "Strengths Finder", and more. I have found the Kolbe A Index to be the most revealing when it comes to entrepreneurs and business.

Finding out your "score" doesn't tell us everything we need to know. However, we must combine that behavioral knowledge with our skills, experience, and practical applications of what it is we do and the industry we work within. Identifying what you do, how you do it, and what you are inclined to do matters. A person who is attracted to systems and processes and feels better crunching numbers on a spreadsheet is not the person you look to drive innovation in the organization.

Knowing your strengths and learning to embrace them and exploit them will help you rise to more success — don't fight what or who you are. We are often taught from an early age to focus on enhancing our strengths. However, kids, students, and often adults who become narrowly focused and "obsessed" with specialization are ostracized. They are considered out of touch with everyone else, or ignorant of what others are doing or feeling. The words "well-rounded" have become a compliment in the highest regard, while one could argue that it basically means average, or status quo. To be well-rounded in a social context is probably a good quality; in fact, it is a huge advantage in life, generally. But when it comes to what you do best, specialization is incredibly valuable.

I will say that I am most definitely a poster child for jack of all trades, master of none. I was very good at everything growing up. I was good at sports, good at music, good at school, I had many friends. I never focused on and developed those specific areas I had real talent for — mostly because I couldn't figure out what might be my real talent. I would say I was an achiever ... not an overachiever. For this I wish I might have done something differently.

Recently I was speaking to my daughter, Madison about her grades. Up until just five years ago, I would have told her she needed to get good grades in every subject. That she needed to excel across the board. While it is still a goal that she achieve decent marks in all subjects, I most certainly have let her know that I would much rather see her strive to get 90%s in her best subjects then try to move her low 70%s to higher 70%s. Think of the difference and perception of her if she achieves improvements of 10% in two subjects. One she is merely good at and the other where she excels. If her 72% in social studies rises to 79%, she is still not honors in that subject, yet if she has an 85% in language arts and her improvement takes her grades over 93%, then she gets noticed, commended, and selected for more opportunities to become excellent in the areas that come natural to her or those which she is passionate about so she can achieve more success.

TAKE THE KOLBE A INDEX — WHAT'S YOUR SCORE?

WHAT IS IT THAT YOU ARE PARTICULARLY GREAT AT?

WHAT OTHER UNIQUE OFFERING DO YOU HAVE TO OFFER (YOUR GREATEST SKILL OR STRENGTH) THAT OTHERS MIGHT NOT?

SECRET TIP 12

> "
> squeeze your niche,
>
> or for my American friends,
>
> squish your niche :)
> "

Embrace the uniqueness of your business and your vision. The closer you move to your unique offering or ability, the more attractive you become. Sounds a bit counterintuitive, right? You'd think if you were more average, more common, with a larger reach, you'd have more sales...that can be correct, but it also brings the lowest common denominator, the biggest headaches and most often, the lowest margins.

A race to the bottom is a race not worth winning.

Specialty and niche businesses scream value. There is a higher premium to be gained. A few less clients paying more and complaining less is a good thing. Also, the further you squeeze into your unique offering the deeper the customer relationships can be. This can also be done on a large scale. BMW, Mercedes, Apple, and the Four Seasons go to great lengths to differentiate themselves from their competitors. Real or perceived it works. They act like and make the claim that they are unique and therefore special. Their marketing goes out of its way to show that. As a result they build a sort of cache and people pay more and value their products above others.

Want to know why more businesses aren't doing this? The first reason is fear. The fear is that you will lose or alienate current customers and there won't be enough new ones to make up for that perceived loss. The second is that it requires a dogged belief that what you are offering will be desired by your future customers. The belief is that what you offer has tremendous value and that there are people who think the same and who will buy from you regardless of what your competitors are doing, or what the market says is "normal". This is not something that can be measured in quarterly reports and sometimes takes time, money, and effort. Once you have squeezed hard enough and built a business that supplies true value to a niche customer, your competitors are few and far between.

Seek blue oceans. This is not a new concept. Professor W. Cahn Kim and Renee Mauborgne made a great breakthrough in using this metaphor to describe this opportunity. Swimming in red oceans is swimming with the sharks — with blood in the water. Your competitors want to eat you, in fact, your customers can't even see you through the proverbial blood and you spend all your time treading water, hoping to survive then die a slow death...when you should be swimming freely. The reason people use multiple products, multiple contractors, multiple advisors and believe their eggs would be better off in many undifferentiated baskets, is because they can't tell the difference. The blue ocean is where you swim to stand out. You are alone and available to those who appreciate your vision and buy what you offer.

WHAT DO YOU ALREADY DO THAT IS UNIQUE?

HOW CAN YOU 'SQUEEZE'
YOUR UNIQUE OFFERING EVEN MORE?

WHERE IS YOUR BLUE OCEAN?
WHERE ARE YOU SWIMMING RIGHT NOW?

SECRET TIP 13

" be talented –
do the
extra work "

I had the joy of listening to the NBA's LA Clippers assistant coach at the time, Kevin Eastman; speak to my mastermind group in February of 2014. Kevin was working with famous coach Doc Rivers at the time and had moved with Doc from the Boston Celtics. A team they guided to the World Championship a few years prior. Kevin, now Vice President of Basketball Operations for the Clippers, was sharing the wisdom he had gained from observations of top performers he had worked with over the years, and landed on a very interesting topic. That topic was talent. We were sitting in a room full of entrepreneurs who had talent and they competed daily in business with others who also have talent. In Kevin's mind there is a clear distinction about those who have talent and those who are talented. He used his observations about Kevin Garnett, one of the NBA's biggest and most dominant stars of the last decade, to illustrate his point. He said while other pros had talent, Kevin Garnett was talented. He spoke of a particular late season practice. Garnett, who had been working extremely hard and needed some rest ahead of a string of important games, was running the normal drills that the second string and rookies were participating in during an optional practice. The coaches determined he needed rest more than work, and encouraged him to sit out for a while. He declined and kept playing. This went on for a short while and eventually, he was basically forced to stop and allow others to run the drill. A few moments later, everyone could hear the breathing, squeaking of shoes and ball hitting the ground in the distance while they were going through the drill. Eastman looked up and saw Garnett, alone, running the entire drill — end-to-end — full out — against imaginary opponents.

Kevin Garnett is easily one of the greatest NBA players, with incredible talent, yet he was running a basic drill on his own, until he got it right.

What Eastman summarized was that

the talented do what others with talent won't.

They will put in the reps; they will perfect their craft and deliver their absolute best — always. The result of course, is that Garnett gains that slight extra advantage ahead of his competitors and rises above them. He has incrementally more success on the court and has exponentially more success on the pay scale.

What are you doing to rise above all others? What legwork are you putting in to get an advantage? When you are successful, are you doing just a bit more to keep that edge? If you are a successful entrepreneur doing well and making a decent living, you will undoubtedly be surrounded by competitors and peers who also have talent. When you do more and step up your game in practice as well as in the game, you give yourself a chance to rise above your competitors and achieve more. Remember incremental improvements can lead to exponential rewards.

WHAT IS YOUR TALENT?

WHAT MAKES YOU TALENT**ED**?

SECRET TIP 14

" build

a

tribe

"

Give me raving fans — maybe even raving lunatics!!! This is where the daily wisdom of Seth Godin, author, speaker, and marketing guru, rings so true. Godin has long touted building your tribe as the best way to market and sell ideas, goods, and services. This concept is centered in highlighting your unique "thing", putting it out there, attracting like-minded people or those who would benefit from you, and doing it over and over. In time, more and more people who see things the way you do will gravitate to what you were saying or doing. The key as you build your tribe is not to sell them things. You develop and nurture your relationship with your tribe and over time you introduce opportunities or products and services that might be helpful to them or desired by them.

Your tribe is the essence of permission marketing and selling.

They are your biggest advocates and some of the best teachers you might access during your career. The maturation of the internet has given almost everyone a platform to be who they are ... and remarkably, they often find that there are many, many more people who feel just like them. Social media has had a compounding effect on reaching like-minded folks. Building this tribe will give you a platform to share, to help, and to offer — sometimes for sale — things that will benefit them. This permission based marketing platform is powerful. Simple email campaigns work and Linked-In is very effective. Now we're not expecting everyone to write a daily blog ... or even weekly for that matter, but you must learn to communicate and reach those who you wish to work with, learn from, and serve.

Who and where are your tribe?

How are you reaching them?

SECRET TIP 15

"
build

barrièrs
"

Unique processes, offerings or originality will distinguish you from your competitors. Teach your ideal clients, and the audience they are in, how you are different from the others. In my financial advisory business, almost every first meeting I have with a prospect, I hear *"I already have a guy ... but he doesn't do that"*. When we meet for even the very first time, in less than an hour, the difference becomes clear to the prospect. I am the strategic expert; their guy is the tactical implementer — or worse, their so-called "advisor" is actually merely a salesman. Do you know how hard it will be for their advisor to re-position themselves as the strategic advisor? Who do you think the client will be more inclined to seek valuable advice from?

Become more specific about why you do what you do and you become even harder to compete with. I am "Canada's leading strategic legacy planner"... I am a speaker, author of three books, business coach, as well as portfolio manager. Any one or two of these positioning statements elevate my positioning, the combination of all of them erect enormous barriers between me, the strategic financial advisor, and other investment advisors. Niche building further reduces the number of competitors you will have. The only way for my competitors to rise above that positioning is to do it on their own, then add their own unique offering. They really have to do all that I've done and then do more. Once you have gained such positioning, you need to go out and aggressively own that territory. Marketing, blogging, speaking, writing, etc. in your own geographic market are all ways to put distance between you and your closest competitors. Do all of these things and do them often.

My competitors might review my Linked-In profile or read

my speaker bio and get tired thinking of even trying to catch up. You must get there too.

Leave your competitors in the dust. Do more, be more, and build more. Exhaust them…

… and when you achieve your goals, you will be able to take a breather and rethink your next move to your next level, while they are still treading water.

Laziness keeps the majority at bay — there is hard work involved in all this. Have no doubt; it takes effort and determination to be exceptional. That said the distance between your potential and others can be expanded by simply putting in more effective work.

"No successful entrepreneur needs to build barriers to their business when their competitors perceive the effort to compete is far too great."

— Mike Skrypnek

WHAT BARRIERS TO ENTRY HAVE YOU ERECTED BETWEEN YOU AND YOUR COMPETITORS?

HOW LONG DO YOU HAVE BEFORE SOMEONE BREAKS THROUGH TO COMPETE DIRECTLY WITH YOU?

SECRET TIP 16

" deliver more,

do more

"

Brian Tracy is one of the most prolific marketers, book writers, and speakers there is. In a recent Skype interview he had with a good friend of mine, Chris Hamilton, he stated that you must provide a value greater than that which your customer expects — ALWAYS.

This is a tangible expression of being talented. There are small things you can do that are unexpected that make all the difference. Everything from simple gifts to high quality products as well as attentive listening will do the trick. That last point is such a big thing. **Listening.** While I have increased the special unexpected "deliverables" or gifts, I have also always taken great care to simply listen better, provide more insightful input and connect with people more than my peers. Being able to provide one small and simple insight or recalling a personal like or dislike or passion, engages people in a much more meaningful way. It is even more powerful if this is a quality that is beyond the service or product you are providing them.

The gift of an interested and genuine personal connection is more powerful than any trinket.

Take the time to show you have listened and care. The result is added clients and much deeper quality client relationships based on trust and respect.

If you decide to give a physical gift, then you must consider where you hope your customer will use it or where it will be with them. It is important to have your presence take up real estate. The three best places for this include their home, their car and their office. Small and useful gifts can send strong messages on an ongoing basis.

Beyond gifts, doing more for your customers means going the extra mile to provide a memorable and enjoyable experience. Every Four Seasons Hotel staff member is provided a "make things right" budget. This is allotted to EVERY staff member. It is designed to empower the staff to immediately and unilaterally make a decision to act to make things right so a customer will enjoy their stay more, or have a problem solved without seeking approval of a manager. In so many ways Four Seasons is doing more. They are doing more for their employees by giving them autonomy of decisions and responsibility of managing their own small budget and they are blowing the customer away! How many times in a normal stay at some other hotel have you had to wait to get service, or a problem solved?

WHAT 3 SMALL GIFT IDEAS
CAN YOU BESTOW UPON YOUR CUSTOMER?

WHAT EXTRAS WILL YOU BUILD
INTO YOUR PRODUCT OR SERVICE OFFERING?

SECRET TIP 17

> "give impeccable service —
> small surprises
> are a BIG deal"

"We create properties of enduring value using superior design and finishes, and support them with a deeply instilled ethic of personal service. Doing so allows Four Seasons to satisfy the needs and tastes of our discriminating customers, and to maintain our position as the world's premier luxury hospitality company." — Four Seasons website page Service Culture, heading "Who We Are."

"Much admired, and not easily replicated, the Four Seasons culture is firmly grounded in our people — in who we are, what we believe and how we behave. Our goals, beliefs and principles are described in the Four Seasons corporate mission statement."

The Four Seasons Hotel and Resorts chain is arguably one of the best quality hotel experiences you will ever have. Their attention to the customer and making your stay memorable and enjoyable is their priority. Not only do they place the customer first at every turn, they also empower their employees with autonomy to handle customer inquiries and concerns on the spot to "make things right".

The key is to learn and understand what your customers want, what they desire — and give it to them. There is a fine line here between doing the small things and setting a precedent of extra service that you might not hope to continue. You might want to send the message to your customer that you are available and concerned about their urgent dilemma, but responding to that email or answering the phone call on Sunday evening opens the door to abuse. It can be just as effective to set expectations in advance, and then "wow" them in another way without sending the wrong message about your service relationship.

Do the little things and they will make big waves.

My mentor and coach, Scott Keffer, and his staff, managed to send a birthday card to me in Calgary, Alberta, Canada, showing up on the exact day of my birthday from Pittsburgh, PA, USA. I was impressed. Just getting things across the border within a week or two can be challenging. Taking the care to ensure delivery was on time and on date meant a lot to me.

You often hear about the "wow" factor. Well this is something you want your customers to say often. When you deliver something they didn't expect, "wow" is their response. People get complacent about their expectations. Too many times, businesses let them down, so they don't expect much. Sometimes just extending an effort to add a personal touch can surprise and delight. During Christmas of 2013, one of Canada's most innovative and customer friendly airlines, WestJet, took "wow" to another level. They launched a customer appreciation event that was a surprise and a relatively small expense for a carrier during the busiest seasons of the year. On a flight from Toronto to Calgary, guests were treated to an incredible surprise. At the departure gates in Toronto guests were greeted by a kiosk with a TV monitor. On the TV monitor was a live feed with Santa Clause. Santa was asking each guest to insert their boarding pass to check in and while doing so, he asked them what they hoped for, for Christmas. Little did they know "Santa" was in a studio in Calgary — their destination. At the same time, he was taking their gift wishes and linking them with their personal information. Once all the passengers were on the plane, West Jet staffers in Calgary had four and a half hours to go out and buy all the things on their guests' gift list. When the passengers arrived in Calgary, each guest was greeted with their personalized gift. Everything from toys to big screen TV's were given. There were shocked, surprised and touched people who all were genuinely impressed and overwhelmed by the generosity and cleverness of the airline. This was one of the most impressive give backs I have ever seen. I heard about it due to the fact that WestJet launched it online as a viral video and it was a big hit.

IN YOUR PERSONAL EXPERIENCE CAN YOU DESCRIBE
THE LAST TIME YOU WERE 'WOWED'?

WHAT WAY WOULD YOU LIKE TO
'WOW' YOUR CUSTOMERS?

SECRET TIP 18

" create

multiple revenue streams

from your

CORE business "

Building multiple revenue streams from multiple diverse sources has long been discussed by the so-called investment gurus and media. Rich dads didn't get rich with multiple streams of revenue; they got rich doing one thing extremely well, and then diversified their investments to protect their assets. It is a myth that you should somehow be great at many things. Engaging in multiple businesses that are not your niche or expertise is not a recipe for success. Last August, I was sitting in an LA hotel restaurant with a wealthy retired, anesthesiologist I know. She shared her observations of her previous physician partners. Lynette explained to me, that she and her husband, another physician made a very good income, were modest spenders, simply invested all their surplus income over their lives and paid down every debt they had. They were in their early sixties, with no debt and plenty of money to do whatever they liked in their twenty to thirty year retirement. She told me the story of one of her partners, who was in his seventies and still working full time. You see, her business partner had decided that even while he was a successful physician, making a great income in his late fifties, he would become a day trader and real estate investor. He made a serious departure from his expertise in medicine and decided to venture into areas that require significant knowledge to become successful. Additionally, finance and investing are very different mindsets from the sciences and physiology of the medical profession. Well, as you might have expected, the experience wasn't a good one. His day trading racked up regular and significant losses — in fact, Lynette said he would actually be trading from his cell phone in the operating room! He also became highly leveraged on his real estate investments and they all went bust in the recession. With no savings, and no other assets, he pretty much had to work until he was eighty. I have always recommended my clients to diversify their investments, not as an income or business generating activity ... but as a risk management one! I would be their investment specialist; they would focus on their professional expertise. This is especially true for entrepreneurs. Investing in you and your human capital to do what you do well is a smart plan. Focusing on your niche and building your core business as the expert, should be your primary focus. You do "one thing" and you do it exceptionally, but when interest or demand dries up ... or markets shift, your family and lifestyle need security.

This does not mean that you commoditize yourself, or become "Fedex". They have been running a TV commercial where the office manager comes in to see the boss in his large office, and the executive is tattooing himself and beating two chess masters with one hand. The message is simply Fedex does everything, and the impression is that all they do is somehow different. What they're not saying is that they are anything but a delivery company. At its core, Fedex moves stuff extremely well. They can deliver anything, anywhere, anytime, but the fact of the matter is that they have a very single minded focus and that is delivering packages. While being Fedex might be a bit more of a logistical nightmare than you are hoping for, they are a great example. Build on your core and figure out many ways to sell services or products connected directly to that core.

While my peers in the investment industry basically receive a single traditional stream of revenue from their business in the form of trading commissions (or even fees for assets), over the past four years, I was determined to establish multiple revenue streams in my business, such that I would not have to rely on the value of investment accounts as my sole way of recognizing revenue. As of today, I have been able to put at least six methods to generate revenue in place, including annual advisory fees, insurance, hourly consulting fees, planning fees, some commission fees and a host of speaking fees. Additionally, I still receive a small amount from my first published book occasionally.

In summary, many different streams of revenue provide many opportunities to save more money, to pay your bills, to invest more in yourself. When one stream is slow, the others might be able to carry you through. When all of them are working at the same time, it is powerful. There will be periods when everything you offer, you create, and you sell are creating cash flow for you and your family. Your peers will be amazed at how you did it, your competitors will wish they were as successful and you will profit. It all stems from one single core ability or skill.

How you build and leverage multiple ways to sell, package and deliver what you do will determine your long term wealth

– not how many different businesses you can get yourself into.

WHAT IS YOUR CORE SKILL OR BUSINESS?

LIST HOW MANY REVENUE STREAMS
YOU HAVE TODAY FROM THIS CORE BUSINESS?

LIST HOW MANY POSSIBLE REVENUE STREAMS YOU COULD HAVE IN THE FUTURE

SECRET TIP 19

“
put the

pedal

to the

metal
”

Successful entrepreneurs make decisions fast.

They are assertive and move quickly. In fact, to the outsider or even their own employees, it appears they are sometimes rash and impulsive, when they are anything but. What they possess is a predetermined, set criterion for making their decisions. They weigh options and quickly understand the upside and downside risk of an action. They know if they can take on a project, or will be able to find people to do so. Here's a simple list that you can use to make your own quick and critical decisions — ask yourself:

Is this opportunity immediately valuable or will it be a value to my customers in the future?

Is this consistent with our brand?

Can this be done elegantly?

Will this be profitable?

Speed and execution matters most. Dan Sullivan, founder and creator of The Strategic Coach™ program really focuses on this concept for entrepreneurs. My first book, my business processes, and my marketing efforts never would have happened as quickly (if at all) if I hadn't constructed a framework to make such decisions and to be comfortable with moving fast. In my second year of "Coach" this principle empowered me to drive ideas forward. Moving everything 80 percent forward, leaves you with 20 ... of which you then attack to 80 percent and so on. Successful entrepreneurs push ideas forward.

Malcolm Gladwell, in his book *"Blink; The Power of*

Thinking without Thinking", discussed making decisions quickly ... seemingly, in the blink of an eye. The reality is that those who can act fast have a skill for "thin-slicing" information and have already established a strong understanding of the decision at hand and the underlying variables. They are just able to filter all this better than most people. It is a skill that can be learned and is a huge advantage for those who can do it well.

Close sales fast. Have a repeatable process in place to move people through uninterested, to interested, to buyer. Ensure that all your timely actions are directed toward your ultimate business goals: more sales, more freedom, and more impact. Your strategies should drive everything to a closing where people buy you, your ideas, your services and your products. If you never do this, you never make a dent in this world.

DESCRIBE A SITUATION WHERE YOU WERE PARALYZED

BY YOUR INABILITY TO MAKE A DECISION

DESCRIBE A MOMENT WHEN YOU MADE

A QUICK DECISION THAT HAD POWERFUL RESULTS

LIST FIVE MORE CRITERIA FOR YOU TO DETERMINE

BEFORE YOU ENTER INTO A DECISION

TO ADVANCE YOUR BUSINESS

SECRET TIP 20

" be

passionate "

Loving what you do makes the doing enjoyable.

People are attracted to those who have passion about their work.

Passion is defined in artistry and craftsmanship and it is respected. Uncover your passion and express yourself. Show passion to your customers, your family, and to yourself and your ideas. Live with passion and embrace the energy it provides, but keep a clear mind and don't fall in love with your passion if no one else will buy it. Leading with passion can produce great outcomes. Paul Alofs, the President of Canada's HMV enterprise in the early nineties, had had a vision for the music industry and successfully carried HMV Music through the changing times in the retail music industry and the company increased its revenue from $30 million to $200 million. In his book, *"Passion Capital"*, Alofs quantified passion as energy plus intensity plus sustainability. He went on to describe seven basic principles to which passion must be applied to generate a spark and wrote that passion capital is the foundation upon which all other forms of capital are built. I largely agree with Paul and ultimately believe that without passion there is nothing. However, I would suggest a measure of caution for the enthusiastic entrepreneurs in the crowd. Alofs didn't have success simply by being passionate about what he did. He took very measured steps to apply his passion to successful business building principles. Beware; passionate people go broke all the time. It isn't enough to be passionate; you must execute smart, effective, money making ideas well.

Launching this book and coaching project, I shared the ideas I was passionate about with my business coach, James Malinchak. I had been mulling the idea of building niches for entrepreneurs and giving back — two areas I am very passionate about. I wanted what I had a passion for to be right there for everyone to see. I thought I would create a catchy acronym for my program. I called my idea *DYN&MIC* training — *"Dominate Your Niche & Make It Count"*. I sat with James in his home and he asked me to explain this in 30 seconds... well, I began some long winded explanation about how niche building is powerful and entrepreneurs need to learn this and when they become rich they can give the money back. All this might be true, but boy did my explanation land with a thud. I was passionate about this...and it was clear no one would get it. We needed to simplify and clarify. People would never invest their hard earned money in what I couldn't explain — just because I knew it would be good for them. It was then that **Big GROWTH Big IMPACT** was born. That's what I am passionate about. Helping entrepreneurs grow their business, get more freedom for themselves, and give back to their community IS my passion...but I had no idea how to present it. Passion is crucial, but smart passion is beautiful.

WHAT IS YOUR PASSION?

HOW WILL YOU APPLY YOUR PASSION TO YOUR BUSINESS PROCESSES?

GET more freedom

for family

for you and

for life

The number one reason entrepreneurs do what they do is for freedom. Choosing to be an entrepreneur is not a "safe" decision. Starting ventures and growing them is fraught with risk. Cash flow is uncertain, there is no job security, and every month, week, or day brings different challenges and opportunities. With all its difficulties and failures, entrepreneurship also has tremendous rewards — both financially and personally. One of the most important drivers of this pursuit is the promise of freedom that being your own boss offers. It is true, entrepreneurs set their own hours, make decisions that weigh their business ambitions with their lifestyle, and have the flexibility to move in any direction they choose. Freedom can be described as having more time. What that means is different for everyone. For some, more time is just that, more time available away from work. For others, it might mean more time to do what they love to do — in work or leisure. We all know as entrepreneurs that the ideal is sometimes hard to achieve. I hear more from entrepreneurs who spend 40, 50, or 80 hours per week working in their business! Their utopia hasn't been realized and they work deep in their business more than working "on" it. This is not a prison sentence and there are those who have mastered strategies to gain their freedom. The following nineteen secrets are tips that successful entrepreneurs have used to achieve freedom, enjoy an exciting and prosperous work life and a fulfilling personal lifestyle.

SECRET TIP 1

" select

the right

people "

Our survey showed that the top concern for entrepreneurs is more sales, but the reason we become entrepreneurs is for more freedom. In a sense it is more time, yet it is really having the freedom to focus on the things you hope to focus on, your passions. It is the freedom to manage your time and spend it how you desire — with family, with friends, for yourself.

When you elaborate on what "more time" means, practically, in business, the conversation almost always moves toward people.

Having enough and having the right ones. Have you ever said this? "If only I had the right person doing (**fill in your biggest challenge here**), I could spend more time doing the things that I love and increase revenue for my business".

When hiring it is important to understand the qualities of the person you wish to hire. These intangibles are the beliefs and values of people who you will rely on and look to for support as you charge ahead. We all know too well what happens when we hire the wrong people. We know it intuitively and quickly, yet we tend to be slow to let them go, so our experience is costly — emotionally and financially. Considerable time and energy is spent dealing with the wrong person and money or opportunity is lost in doing so. Just because someone has the right qualities, it doesn't make them a right fit.

Entrepreneurs are visionaries. They also want to share their vision with everyone. Not everyone wants to learn your vision; they aren't motivated by your vision. They might like it and aspire to the ideal, but they aren't driven by it. We hope they are like us because we are looking to be energized, but the qualities we require to provide support for our business are not found in copies of ourselves.

The right people lift you up and allow you freedom. They do not have any need to "be like you". The usual perception of a lack of time is really your view on the lack of time to spend doing the things that energize you. The right people working with you and for you will change your view of this. There is a famous African saying quoted heavily around the world in business and that is: *"If you want to go fast, go alone. If you want to go far, go together."* While an entrepreneur is alone in many ways — unique vision, unwavering determination, and acceptance of risk, they are never truly successful on their own. Understanding how others fit, how people lift you up and support your vision is critically important. The people you surround yourself with make the difference between success and excellence. In my opinion, it is also the key difference between a stressful and an enjoyable and fulfilling life. Surround yourself with great people, train them, and encourage them and you will gain more freedom than you ever thought possible.

The right people energize you and give you freedom, while those who are not a fit, will cause you to lose your energy restricting your freedom. Remember people you hire will allow you to operate at your best in your "zone" using your unique ability as much as possible.

WHERE AND WHEN DO YOU GAIN YOUR ENERGY?

WHERE AND WHEN DO YOU LOSE YOUR ENERGY?

WHAT FREEDOM DO YOU HOPE TO GAIN
FROM HIRING YOUR NEXT EMPLOYEE?

SECRET TIP 2

" establish a process

to hire

great people "

You know your freedom stems from having great and right people working with you. When hiring it is important to work with people who complement you, as well as challenge you and have skills that are not exactly what you do. We know we want a person with certain qualities and values, in fact we want to like them and we want them to like us and believe in our vision. So the entrepreneur steps into the hiring process. This is inherently challenging. I recommend you always have someone else do the hiring for you, or at the very least, with you. Repeat after me: "*An entrepreneur shall not hire one's own employees' single-handedly.*" Here's why: You are always marketing ... this will include how you conduct your job interview.

Selling the candidate on the role inserts your vision where it is not effective.

Without a process for hiring that has specific and clear criteria, we will very likely make similar wrong decisions in hiring over and over.

How do we build our process and list of criteria we hope to have in a new employee? Well, you start at the same point any effective marketing program would...you ask the target customer what they need and want. I recommend you identify two or three employees you admire who work with other leaders in the same industry. In order to learn from them to better understand how your potential candidate thinks, interview them. Consider them the ideal candidate working elsewhere. Have simple questions about motivation, happiness, compensation, and work related questions focusing on what they like to do or what they would rather avoid. You will learn a LOT!

When I needed to hire my next assistant, I spent an hour interviewing an associate whom I admired and thought would be a great addition to my team. I was never going to hire her away from her employer — whom I respected — but I certainly wanted to learn what was important to her in her role so I could tailor my hiring approach to the person I needed. I asked her what her ideal day looked like, what motivated her to perform, and asked her about her thoughts on fair compensation. Very much unlike me, she stated that she valued security and consistency both in her daily routine and her compensation. She preferred task oriented bonuses rather than growth ones. Additionally, she valued time even more than financial rewards for meeting or exceeding performance targets. Naturally this was quite an eye opener for me. If it was up to me, I would have structured the role and my hiring process to reflect my values and the things that motivated me as an entrepreneur. It became clear to me why I was so unsuccessful at hiring in the past.

While building your ideal candidate role, you must be able to clearly articulate specific skills they need to be successful in the role. This helps keep you from selling the position to the candidate. Build the role and job description first and then hire. It is an incredibly significant error to ignore your role description and criteria only to end up hiring someone you really like and want to work with, but doesn't fit the role. Avoid creating the role for the person ... the role comes first, the right person will follow.

Other important criteria to include in your hiring process are qualities such as experience. This will largely depend on the role and will depend on the type of business. Also, there are degrees of experience. In one case you might need an applicant with significant industry specific experience, while in others maybe it is a skill they need, while the type of business experience doesn't matter, as the skill is transferrable. If you offer extensive on-the-job training and prefer to hire individuals with no experience, but have the capacity to learn, then you want to be sure you hire people with intelligence and common sense. Businesses with strong processes and systems in place need smart, energized, and qualified candidates. Everything can be learned or followed.

Other qualities that are important to consider in the hiring process include understanding a person's strengths and their natural tendencies. There are many test or evaluation metrics available to employers these days. I highly recommend you make use of widely available personality testing protocols. They work and they prevent headaches down the road. They also provide much more objectivity for decision making in hiring.

We have used the "Kolbe A Index" and Tom Rath's "Strengths Finder" to get to the heart of how a person will naturally tend to behave and act, and where we might uncover their unique ability. Hiring a likeable person to do marketing, who has incredible academic skills, but is naturally shy and introverted, yet likeable will not likely find success in such a role. This might be common sense, but sometimes isn't so apparent, however I had interviewed a person for an executive assistant role who I liked very much, who had a great resume with a lot of experience and seemed very driven. In fact, I was blown away at how she had spent the past decade learning, advancing, and growing her resume. She was clearly a motivated person. When I reviewed her Kolbe A Index results, I realized I liked her because she was more similar to me in her tendencies and had the success she had because of her motivations. What the test revealed was that she did not score well on her ability to follow through or to dig for facts. These two qualities are extremely important for a high "quick start" marketing type like me. There are optimum "matches" for people with varying scores or profiles. Both Kolbe and Strengths Finder offer guides to how to use their findings in hiring and combining employees.

Lastly, while not every position requires a high level of it, I still recommend you hire for intelligence in conjunction with the other qualities and criteria I have already mentioned. Basic qualities of intelligence (or cognitive ability) can never be underestimated. Certificates and diplomas provide some evidence of baseline intelligence, but can be deceiving. Use a simple intelligence measure to set a baseline for your candidates. I have found that when an employee has higher intelligence and common sense they will be able to more quickly learn and adapt to new concepts and skills. A high common sense IQ reflects someone culturally connected as well. One test that is used by many of people I respect is called the "Wonderlic Cognitive Ability Test". It is focused on aptitude and problem solving abilities. It is a simple 50 multiple choice question test that takes less than 15 minutes.

Whatever types of tests you decide to use, you should make some of them part of the pre-interview process and include some in the interview as well. Setting roles, establishing criteria, and adding these types of tests bring small hurdles to your hiring process. A candidate who decides to complete your process will rise to the top. In fact, they will be only one of a small number who actually get to that point. The process helps you filter a large amount of candidates who would otherwise be wasting your time.

Here's one last word for your new hiring process. Don't allow yourself to accommodate a poor showing for any reason. When you really like a person and the same candidate believes they are well qualified, they may show a less than high standard — while simply positioning it as them being more "casual" or personal. Formality and achievement are measurable qualities and they are indicators of pride in work, attention to detail, and understanding of importance. When you accommodate a lower performance level and establish low expectations, the standard is set. Subsequently, you will be disappointed with the results. Raise the bar very high up front and you can always soften your stance in time with the right employee. Trying to raise your game AFTER you've set the tone will not work.

CREATE A DETAILED DESCRIPTION OF THE ROLE OR THE POSITION YOU ARE TRYING TO FILL

WHAT ARE THE VALUES AND QUALITIES OF PEOPLE YOU HOPE TO WORK WITH?

WHAT LEVEL OF EXPERIENCE WILL YOU REQUIRE?

WHAT TESTS WILL YOU ASK CANDIDATES TO TAKE?

SECRET TIP 3

" *invest the time and energy into processes to train the right people the right way* "

———————•———————

Your new employee has successfully gone through a number of steps that you have asked them take to be hired. You have spent time and energy already in finding the right person. Everyone is excited and ready to move forward. On the first day, you walk the new employee around your office and introduce them to everyone. You show them the kitchen and the copy room and their workstation. They turn on the phone and computer, and then you promptly head to your office or a meeting to get on with your typically busy day. Along the way, you request certain tasks to be completed and point them toward steps you hope for them to take. Later on the same day, as you pass by them, you rattle off some inaudible instructions and go on to your next task. This persists for a month and things seem to be going okay, until the day that you demand a report or task completed and it is not done right, nor on time. You then consider that maybe the new hire is not quite right for the position. Maybe you missed something when you hired them, or maybe they're just not up to the task. From that point on, failings are exaggerated and shortcomings are glaring. They get frustrated and you want them gone. The problem is ... it was your entire fault. You brought a quality person on to your team and left them blowing in the wind to fend for themselves. This could have gone worse. The new employee could have miscommunicated with a customer or blown a sale.

To avoid this, you must care for them, nurture them and train them. They are your best assets and they are the face of your company or the backbone of it. Either way, you hired them to give you more freedom, more peace of mind and to increase your capacity to do your thing. If these goals are why your hired the person, it is critical that you spend time training them and set them up for success.

Properly run and successful businesses invest money and time in training their people well. Don't leave anything to chance.

YOUR reputation is at risk. You write the scripts, design the processes and goals. Give tools to them and instruct them how to use them to achieve success in their work. Then MEASURE and evaluate them! Improve them and repeat.

Do you use any of the following training tools?

▶ PROCESS MANUALS

▶ SCRIPTS

▶ ROLE PLAYING

▶ MENTORSHIP

▶ PRACTICE AND REHEARSAL

▶ EVALUATION AND CRITIQUE

SECRET TIP 4

" surround yourself
with like-minded people
and positive influences "

Hiring the right people is an important investment in your business. They will be those who support you and the business. They will not typically be the people who are the same as you, or motivate and inspire you. This is just fine; they are there to help you run your business more effectively. You will develop relationships with your employees in different ways, but you won't likely be getting together for Sunday dinner, or in a social setting.

In your personal life and work life, hang out and seek guidance and collaboration with people who energize you. This is about **energy and growth**, NOT building marketing networks or staffing.

People who can inspire you, push you and motivate you will raise you up. Surround yourself with them.

Join masterminds or build advisory committees and participate in roundtables. Napoleon Hill (Think and Grow Rich) introduced the idea of mastermind groups over fifty years ago. I have participated in many such groups for years and will continue to do so. A mastermind group is a collection of like-minded people meeting regularly with the intent to help each other achieve success by sharing insights and knowledge. It is often an environment where a break-through can be made for business growth or to resolve a challenge presented by a member of the group. The collective wisdom of the group raises the level of problem solving and brainstorming. The benefits from mastermind groups range from sharing accountability to gaining invaluable ideas to building a sense of community. Smart people, enthusiastic people, and positive people bring a ton to the table. Input from like-minded people who do different things than you gives great insight in problem solving for your business.

Why do we become entrepreneurs? To get more freedom. What is the meaning of freedom? It means spending more time and energy working in your zone and developing your personal and interpersonal relationships. Mastermind groups give you this and more. They allow you incredible freedom to expand your thinking. They improve your sense of community in all you do and the energy that comes from such brainstorming is amazing. Knowing that others think like you and can help you as well as you can help them is stimulating. When you are energized and confident, you are happier. When you're happier and inspired you improve the life of those around you and you will have more meaningful interactions with friends and family.

How do you mastermind? Well, you can join already established mastermind groups or you establish your own. Often business coaching groups will also organize groups within their coaching members. Before you go throwing the idea around spontaneously, please know that this is an investment. It is an investment in your business and your personal growth. You must invest your time and attention. This is something you must do often. Two to four times per year is what you should schedule for your group. There might be a financial investment if travel is required to meet, or if there are other educational aspects offered by the organizer or coaching group. What I know is the ideas, the personal joy, and the financial benefits you gain from participating regularly in a mastermind are exponentially more than what you put in.

DO YOU PARTICIPATE IN A MASTERMIND GROUP?

IF YOU ARE NOT IN A MASTERMIND GROUP NOW,
NAME FIVE OTHER PROFESSIONALS YOU KNOW
WHO YOU WOULD LIKE TO
SHARE, LEARN, AND GROW WITH

WHEN WILL YOU START YOUR NEW
MASTERMIND GROUP?

SECRET TIP 5

" *read*

to

succeed

"

———•———————•———

"Read at every wait; read at all hours, read within leisure, read in times of labor. The task of the educated mind is simply put."

– Cicero

Dave (aka "Famous Dave") Anderson, a Native American Indian, grew up poor in inner city Chicago. I was in the audience at a boot camp in Los Angeles and heard Dave tell his story. It was incredibly moving and inspiring. Dave is a living testament to why "readers" succeed. In elementary school, Dave's teacher asked for students to approach the front of the class to answer a question at the blackboard. Dave raised his hand to answer, but the teacher stopped him and cruelly stated, "You're too dumb to answer the question, David. Let someone else who is smarter, answer it." This hurt deeply and stuck with him for his entire life. When he was growing up his family ran a food concession stand at Powwows on the nearby Indian reserve. Dave's thing was Barbeque. He loved it and loved cooking it and selling it. This is where his vision for Famous Dave's BBQ was born — and now there are over 170 Famous Dave's restaurants across the USA. He also knew that he would need an education to succeed in business — a spectrum where he was completely naive. So he read. He read and read and read. His knowledge base expanded and his business did too ... as did his wealth. While there have been many ups and downs in his life, Dave said that one of the biggest financial shocks he had ever had was "losing" $80 million in a week when the stock market tanked in 2008. Years prior to that, his other more personal shock was the day his family staged an intervention to help bring him out of his spiralling addiction. In short order, but not without serious hard work and commitment, Dave has fully recovered from those hardships. What I found astounding was the picture he showed the audience of his library ... or rather the new "wing" of his library. It was his garage — with crates of books and shelves stacked to the ceiling with books he had read. He had to move his library out to the garage after the one in his house was packed to the rafters! In his mid-thirties, Dave achieved his Master's degree from Harvard — with NO undergraduate degree — a testament to his mantra of read, read, read. Dave connects his success to reading.

Reading gives the entrepreneur freedom by opening up the world to unrestrained information and opportunity.

All you know is what you learn, what you learn is what you experience and read. Dedication to reading will expand your mind and increase your wealth.

WHAT ARE YOU READING RIGHT NOW?

HERE'S A LIST YOU MIGHT WANT TO CONSIDER

Think and Grow Rich – Napoleon Hill

Tipping Point – Malcom Gladwell

Money Well Spent – Paul Brest & Hal Harvey

No BS Time Management for Entrepreneurs – Dan S. Kennedy

7 Habits of Highly Effective People – Stephen R. Covey

Purple Cow – Seth Godin

Millionaire Success Secrets – James Malinchak

Good to Great – Jim Collins

Open – Andre Agassi

Onward – Howard Schultz

SECRET TIP 6

" read to learn
HOW TO DO things and
what TO AVOID
"

Within the wisdom of books lie answers to almost anything you hope to know or wish you could master.

Success is found in the collective wisdom of the written word. Not only is reading inspiring, it can provide you the most fundamental step-by-step learning there is. While reading has expanded my thinking and enriched my life, what I have learned from reading is HOW to do things. Within all books I have read, there are secrets or signs and even straight out instructions on how to do everything. In the pages of books, the steps are all there!

The greatest minds of history and the most successful people there ever were, have written books or had books written about them. Their wisdom is shared for all to learn. Buy their books, download their audio book, or simply go to the library and read them.

This book is a compilation of knowledge gleaned from successful people and also with wisdom learned from my firsthand experiences. Other books can be quite specific from "How to close sales to dentists" to "How to build great hiring processes for IT professionals". The "For Dummies" series is a perfect example of the specific "How to" manuals for everything.

Reading to learn how will give you the freedom of knowledge. Learned knowledge obtained from reading is knowledge you have forever. Once learned, you can move on to the next thing. Reading allows an entrepreneur to learn how to do things before they learn the hard way. The biggest piles of stinking stuff have been simply, thankfully, mapped out for you. Naturally there are experiences that are worth enduring ... most bad ones are not. Those who have been there before can point out the time and money wasters — read their words and take heed!

It is not a pre-requisite of success to make all the mistakes yourself. You will undoubtedly make a lot of them as you move forward, but there are smarter, more successful people than you who have made bigger, dumber, and costlier mistakes than you will ever make — and you can read about them to learn how to avoid them. For everyone there is an investment in learning on your own and from others. It is part of the process. There are great books that will teach you the potholes to step around ... and it will be less expensive to do so. The freedom you will bring to your life and business through reading is priceless.

WHAT DO YOU WISH TO LEARN?
DO A BOOK, DON'T JUST READ IT!

WHICH SUCCESSFUL ENTREPRENEURS DO YOU
ADMIRE? OR NAME YOUR TOP TEN LIST OF HIGHLY
SUCCESSFUL PEOPLE YOU MOST ADMIRE.

WHAT FIVE THINGS
DO YOU WANT TO LEARN FROM THEM?

SECRET TIP 7

" establish processes

for

EVERYTHING "

Processes give those who are not like you and do not think like you a road map to success. Your employees require clear guidance and repeatable processes to guide them in delivering services and support.

Well defined processes for executing everything in your business take the guesswork out of your business and build consistency.

They free you up from ad hoc actions and give you a path to learning along the way. The freedom you gain from having processes will be realized in so many ways. You will gain time from having everything laid out for you and your staff. You will build confidence in your staff and your customers, because the discipline that process brings is comforting. As W. Edward Deming once said, "If you cannot describe what you do as a process, you don't know what you are doing". The importance of having processes cannot be understated.

A few years ago, I began to describe an amazing initiative I was about to embark on and how my wife, Sherri, was going to support me. I included the fact that I had committed $20,000 to the program for year one, that I had to present over eight times per year to a variety of audiences, that we had to teach my customers how to administer the program, and that she was to be the liaison for all questions and inquiries from customers of that program. Now, what makes Sherri an excellent partner in life and work is that she processes things very differently than me. She really is the yin to my yang. I was so excited about embarking on this that I forgot just how overwhelming the project could be for her. As I was describing all the aspects, she just stared at me and looked down to review her text messages. It was clear that as I spoke, she got more anxious and soon she was suggesting that maybe she wasn't the right person to handle this with me. I suddenly realized I needed to start speaking her language, and fast. I quickly told her that the program was a step by step program and there would be people to support her and provide her answers to all the questions she might have. While that helped, it didn't quite do the trick. I then stacked four stuffed program binders onto her desk — I had been avoiding reading them, because when I saw all the pages, I basically got a bit overwhelmed. When she started leafing through the binders, she quickly realized every single step and every last detail were carefully outlined — down to the seating arrangements and placement of materials for our client presentations...even how to fold the brochures (things I really didn't want to be bothered with). She loved it! She breathed an enormous sigh of relief and immediately became engaged and happy. When she learned that everything, right down to the scripts for conversation, as well as the precise timing of steps was provided, she was elated. In fact, while I found it rather conforming and too detailed for my liking, she found the whole thing liberating. Your employees do not think like you. They appreciate process. Give them process, allow them to focus on the details.

Process gives you scalability. When you have processes in place to handle your business, you can handle much more than you did before and you can do it better. When everyone in your organization is scrambling to find solutions and making things up as they go, a lot of time is wasted. Their capacity to handle more volume is diminished.

Process gives you freedom. When you are away from the day to day of the business, you are able to relax, knowing your employees will all follow their known guidelines and that all customers and situations will be dealt with in a standardized manner. You are free to think about bigger picture things, or free to step away without worry for your personal time.

The last thing I would remind you about process is that YOU must be the one who builds the outline of how things should be done. This is your business, your vision, and your reputation. Don't leave anything to chance. This means spending time up front in establishing your processes including scripting of communications with clients, marketing messaging, and sequential activities.

HERE'S A HELPFUL TIP: Audio record all that you do, in a specific sequence of customer service, or communications or marketing and have it transcribed. Clean it up and presto ... you have your manual. Do this for every area in your business.

DO YOU HAVE PROCESSES IN PLACE
FOR EVERY ASPECT OF YOUR BUSINESS?

CAN YOU DESCRIBE WHAT YOU DO AS A PROCESS?

SECRET TIP 8

"
outsourcing
"

Hire, for less, what you can't and shouldn't do for yourself.

Using the internet and the broad online world of educated people and capable resources available today, you can pretty much expand your capacity exponentially. However, if you do not know what you are doing, you can end up investing money learning a lot of who not to hire or what to pay for. Online services like Elance, or Fiver, have writers, graphic artists, web designers, etc. They all compete in a global online marketplace for your business. It is cost effective and simple. However, a major drawback can be lost in translation — quite literally. Sometimes the quality low cost professionals are from all over the globe. If your project requires conveying your vision or a message to a specific and local demographic, you might find the cultural nuances can be lost when you see the finished project. It will very likely be on time and on budget ... but in some ways, you'll find it might not be quite right. You should apply similar processes to hiring "elancers" as you would employees and contractors. Leverage high quality resources, without placing them on staff, and focus on what you do best.

My good friend, John Leishman, founder of Tursa Group and outsourcing master, has changed online staffing and outsourcing for everything from bookkeeping to writing to website development. He has combined web-based infrastructure, cloud technology, and cost-efficiency with Skype-based communication tools and culturally knowledgeable support for each project. I have managed to have websites completed, Skype-interviews, online surveys, and other marketing initiatives among a number of other services performed. John's model is truly awesome.

DO YOU OUTSOURCE TASKS
IN YOUR BUSINESS TODAY?

WHAT ASPECTS OF YOUR BUSINESS
WOULD YOU LIKE TO OUTSOURCE?

SECRET TIP 9

" hire

coaches & mentors and

attend masterminds

"

———————

Top performers know this, top athletes know this, the best singers and actors know this, the top ten CEOs and entrepreneurs in North America will tell you they have mentors and coaches.

The top business professionals work in mastermind groups. They share big ideas with others like them. They network and learn firsthand from others' experiences. The best athletes, the top singers and actors all have coaches. What happens when a golfer wants a few strokes off his game? He hires a coach and practices. The coach can see things the golfer does not. They have a working expertise in connecting the dots. Their objective eye can identify areas for improvement as well as push for further growth in places where a little support can be the difference in moving to another level. The training coaches have had, under the tutelage of other successful coaches provided them firsthand knowledge of their craft. They are able to synthesize ideas and apply objectivity.

What is the value of a business breakthrough to you? How much would you invest to learn how to predictably attract a steady stream of ideal clients? How would you like to learn about the things that you do all the time that might be holding you back?

The people you work with won't give you strong constructive critical feedback, but a coach will be straight with you when you need it.

You invest in them to pull you through these things. There are so many things a coach will bring — in fact, a good or great coach can be a fountain of ideas and information that you might use. The variety of input can be overwhelming at times, so I recommend applying your coaching knowledge in the way that you would eat an elephant ... one small bite at a time. One good idea from a coach can make all the difference. For a pro basketball player working on free throws, it could be simply keeping their elbow in. For a singer it could be the way they are breathing that will improve their tone. For an entrepreneur it could be directing their attention to scripting communications. It is that ONE THING ... that makes all the difference.

I was working with a coach a few years ago. When I went to visit him for an intensive one-on-one session, I was brimming with all kinds of ideas and goals. I had new initiatives I wanted to discuss as well as ideas I had for future projects on my mind. But there was one key problem, I was over worked and couldn't focus on business building because I was focused on carrying freight in my business. I hadn't done too well to hire quality employees who I could trust to "mind the store" while I was away working on growth. I was also trying to skimp on paying a newly hired employee in the process, as cash flow was tight. My coach stopped my grandiose ideas in their tracks and brought me back to the present moment, and helped me focus on two key things — stabilizing my cash flow and hiring the "right fit" employee. The decision to concentrate on my hiring process to get the exact right person in place was powerful. He showed me a road map to get that done — a lot of what I have shared previously in this book. Within six months, I had two right fit employees working with me, both of whom have been a great investment. They have given me time and energy to focus on the things that energize me and grow my business. The wisdom of coaches and mentors will SAVE YOU TIME!

They might save you years in development or they might drive you to focus on a specific goal which could grow your business exponentially. The freedom you get from crucial time-saving help is a very tangible and key benefit.

Another way coaches help you is by raising the bar for higher achievement. I would say this is one thing I have directly experienced in working with my first coaching customer. When I began working with Michael, he was struggling to figure out ways to increase his annual membership model for online training. He had done so much work on building his platform and recording online tutorials and courses. The product was good, but he wasn't totally focused on the marketing and sales. He had about $60,000 in sales the prior year and had only been attracting four or five new members per month. He was focused on building more and more products for those users, was working on programming, website development, and bookkeeping over 70% of his time and only focusing on marketing for about 15% to 20% of his time. His number one requirement was to keep his wife and children living in their home and enjoying a good lifestyle — but he was lacking sales. I quickly set to work with him restructuring his membership model, and re-focusing his time on marketing and sales. He was moving outside his comfort zone, and I knew it — but he had no choice. In order to grow we had to give him the tools to make selling more natural and to have it stay top of mind at all times. Within three months, he was tracking at twice the number of registrations as before and was on track to double his annual sales.

This past summer I urged him to take on applying in an RFP process, that he was a peripheral player in, with a major company which would have had him provide training to hundreds of their employees and secure a sizeable three year contract. He was about to meet them for a follow up session in person — something prior to the process he thought was beyond him. There was one hitch. They asked him to arrive in Las Vegas to present just one day prior to the day he and his wife were to leave for a ten day vacation in France. He was about to back out and we were having one of our regular calls. I urged him to find a way to get there. He could rest on the flight home and to Europe. When we got off the phone, I wasn't sure if he would actually commit to Vegas.

I hadn't heard from him for a few weeks and when we spoke again, he informed me that he had followed my instructions and prepared and travelled to Vegas to present. They had since asked him for more information and to move to the last round of the process. His more comprehensive proposal for this potential contract also grew. The financial upside ballooned to a possible one million dollars! If the company finds his unique positioning to be attractive, he might just get a shot at training their hundreds of employees.

As I wrote this, he was waiting to hear back from the company. He has a real shot at obtaining the largest contract of his career. This is freaking him out! In a way, he said, he does not want to win the RFP. It would mean a huge change to his life, increased pressure, frequent travel, and deadlines. All negatives. On the upside, the achievement would launch his credibility, and allow him to attract high quality contracts from now on. Finally, the money would be a major positive development for his family. But he remained fearful. As his coach, I am working through this with him. We will tackle his fears. We will address how to overcome his concerns and construct a more manageable framework to embrace the success.

I feel a great deal of responsibility for his growth in tackling projects and opportunities he never would have considered. It is exciting what can happen when you take people beyond their own mental constructs to places they can have great success, but didn't fathom. My coaches and so many others do this regularly. Their objectivity expands your mind. This unrestrained thinking gives you freedom to be more and achieve more than you thought possible.

WHO DO YOU CONSIDER A MENTOR?

DO YOU HAVE A COACH?

HOW HAS YOUR COACHING EXPERIENCE BEEN?

DO YOU MASTERMIND? IF YES, HOW OFTEN?

GET more freedom

SECRET TIP 10

" protect

your

time

"

Dan S. Kennedy is a master at this. In fact, you could say he wrote the book on it. One of his many "No B.S." books focuses on time management. He suggests you start by measuring what your time is worth to you, and then fiercely protect it. Every time you spend time on things that are not productive take an inventory and value them against your worth — more simply, your hourly rate or value. This requires establishing gatekeepers — people and systems to manage. It is possible to do this on your own, but it will be even more effective to train others to assist you.

In the first day of Strategic Coach™, you are taught the basic principles of time blocking. Segmenting your time in to money making (focus days), business building (buffer days), and personal regeneration (free days) time. This is not the perfect system, but it is a pretty good one. If anything, it gets you paying more attention to segmenting time to handle the needs of an entrepreneur. Performing at your best when you are "on stage" requires preparation and energy. The buffer and free days give you this, so you are able to be at your best.

We don't work to become slaves to our business. Too often we are working "in" our businesses, not on them.

In order to grow and thrive, you need to spend more time thinking about your business and planning for the next big opportunity.

While this is obviously beneficial, it is often time which entrepreneurs never invest. Typically, plowing forward with little side tracks or contemplation leaves less to be achieved. Without great thinking there are no great ideas. Not investing the time for this cheats you and those around you. Work, thought, and personal time are equally important. You must also make time for you and your family. If you let your personal time slide, then you are risking the most important things in life.

If interviewed and asked to summarize one's life at the end of their time on earth, it would be safe to say that not one person would ever have regrets that they should have worked harder, or put one more hour in the office. They will always lament the time they didn't spend with family or doing things that are important to them. We all have the same finite amount of time each day. Protect it fiercely and enjoy it.

Do you block time in your schedule?

If yes, how do you do it?

Be honest, have you been

effective at protecting your time?

SECRET TIP 11

" *schedule*

your time and

all your appointments "

Freedom equals time. Time is precious for you, your family and your business. If you are losing time throughout your day, attending to wasteful activities that extend your work day, or diminish your effectiveness, then you are allowing an intrusion into your personal and family time. You must protect your time unapologetically. This section is about managing your time and limiting wastefulness. The next point will cover how to maximize the use of your time.

Scheduling everything in your business days is the first place to start. Create a schedule for your days each week to focus on making money, to think, and to rejuvenate. In order to do this, you must block your time. You might ask, how you can do this when your customers, or staff want and need you desperately. Well, the first thing you need to understand is that they'll be fine without you for a while. The second thing is that they will be much better off with you completely focused on them during a set appointment time that you will be attentive to their needs or concerns exclusively. Contrary to your hard wired belief, or rather "always on" compulsion,

scheduled appointments show respect for customers and your employees as opposed to being some kind of dismissive message.

Six years ago, I moved to having all my client reviews scheduled quarterly. This was a monumental shift for me and my business. In the past, all the customers I worked with were used to unscheduled calls and ad hoc meetings, I was "always available", and anything could happen at any time. I felt like a slave to my work and began to feel contempt for my clients who were "barging" into my day. I took every call, because I was also concerned they would think that somehow by being unavailable I might be ignoring them or their phone calls or emails. I didn't get much productive work done and the best I could do was react. To my detriment, I got so good at behaving this way, that some days, all I would do is wait for the calls to come in — it was too exhausting to build a plan for the day and have it constantly interrupted so I would simply react to everything. Guess what? It became so frustrating I began to hate most of those days. My customers weren't getting the best of me; they were merely getting my reactions. I was doing nothing strategic to help them.

When I changed this and began to schedule my time, some of my customers didn't like it. It took a while for me to stay committed to this ... and even today I still work at it. I am always reducing my list of people who have unfiltered access, but it is still probably too big. Ideally this should be reserved for top customers, energizing people, and family.

By setting a quarterly schedule process, my primary goal at the time was to standardize my customer portfolio review and contact. A number of positive side effects have resulted. The first is now my year is now broken into four three-month segments with consistent themes: Month one — Q reviews, Month two — follow up and implementation, Month three — business development and education/training. Early on, the hardest thing for me was to get used to my own perception of nothing happening during the business development month. I had wrongly grown so conditioned to believe that the only time I was working effectively was when I was on the phone with customers. What really happened when I became committed to scheduling and appointments was that I was able to work on bigger projects and more strategic marketing. I had to also learn that when this was the case, there weren't immediate results for the bigger planning. Those strategic efforts take longer to create meaningful results. I still find I get a bit unsettled during the planning months. That said; I have become better at accepting this once the results began to shine through.

The second side effect of this formal scheduling was the incredible power of connectedness that has improved my customer relationships. What a relief! The predictable, consistent scheduling process instills confidence and anticipation for my customers. They are now very responsive to scheduling and are more prepared when we speak. Our conversations are more productive.

Thirdly, due to the nature of our structured agenda, we cover many more details about my customer's life and financial situation than in the past ... some conversations simply enhance our relationships, while other conversations lead to more revenue generating, planning, and implementation opportunities.

Finally, because the conversations are more in depth, there is minimal need to connect between quarters. I am freer to work on strategic planning and thinking...something that was almost impossible when I was reacting.

So how do you put this into action? Well, you must assign the role of gatekeeper to someone you trust with such a role. They typically, but not necessarily, will be your executive assistant. They are in charge of protecting you and your time. Ideally, you will have them answer all your incoming phone calls, review and filter your email, and most definitely stop all unscheduled "walk-in" meetings.

This person will also be the person who schedules every appointment, call, or meeting. They will be your voice of reason when you feel compelled to do any one of these things above. They will remind you that it is not good use of your time. Give them the authority to do this. You will appreciate the intervention. I would suggest even to give them the veto on some of your time wasting endeavours. Entrepreneurs get distracted from time to time and take on tasks, or roles that might be interesting to us, yet will drain us of time and energy. These things are disguised as favors, requests to "pick your brain", and invitations such as "let me buy you coffee". If you hear the following, run! "I was wondering if I could get your opinion on something ..." Your gatekeeper will see this better than you sometimes and thus are in a good position to gently remind you that maybe your time is better spent focusing on your core business. They will help you say "NO".

DO NOT take ad hoc calls, meetings, or conversations during your working hours. These things burn your time faster than polyester pants near a blazing campfire. Poof! Just watch your day go up in smoke. Attending meetings, unless they are customer facing or for strategic planning and implementation, is a complete waste of time and you must avoid them at all costs. How many meetings have you sat in and wondered to yourself why you accepted the invitation in the first place? Exactly! Stop going to them at once and do not organize them without a clear agenda and a defined time frame. They smash a two hour hole into your previously productive day. Again, avoid at all cost.

WHO IS YOUR GATEKEEPER?

WHAT DAYS WILL YOU FOCUS ON MAKING MONEY, STRATEGIC PLANNING, OR REJUVENATING?

SECRET TIP 12

" limit &

maximize your time —

compulsively
"

———————————

Consistent with the time protection and management theme above is a focus on making the most of the time you have now blocked for yourself. Let's think of this in a bigger context than just your working days, let's add in your personal life time as well. Think of things in this way, during a typical day, there are the same twenty four hours everyone in the world has. We sleep for roughly eight hours, we work for about eight hours, and the other eight hours are spent in personal time; enjoying personal pursuits and family time. That means two thirds of our days are exclusively for us. We must ensure this time is great time and healthy enriching time. We must leave work and stress out of our minds while being fully present with ourselves and our family and friends. But when was the last time you were able to completely disconnect from your work? Not too often, right? This is mostly because entrepreneurs have a nagging sense that they didn't get enough accomplished in their day. That somehow they must carry on until they are done...but we know that never happens because once one project is done, we're on to the next.

Not one person, EVER, on their death bed, suggested they should have worked more hours or they regretted not spending more time at the office…

no, they would have given everything to have another day with their family or enjoying personal activities. I want to give you some ideas on how to manage your work time to improve your personal time. How we can reduce the stress of bringing our work home with us, is by ensuring we maximize our time productively during our work hours. That is the one third of our day in which we devote to building our business, realizing our vision, and of course, making money. There are many ways to become more efficient and more productive — in fact, I am sure most of you who are reading this book already accomplish more in a few focused productive hours than most people would in an entire week of work.

The previous tip discussed how to schedule your time better. This is a critical step to protecting you and your effectiveness. When you are freed up from the chaos of random conversations, ad hoc meetings, phone calls and email distractions, you are able to focus and be more productive. When your mind lets go of the need to take on everything and solve every problem, as it comes along, you become free to think strategically and create. This segment discusses increasing the productiveness of the time you have allotted in your day.

How you use your work time is critical. The first suggestion I have is to set a ritual or routine. This is the series of things you do every day that clear your mind, reduce anxiety, and energize you. Everyone has a different bio rhythm, so how this unfolds each morning is up to you. An hour spent each morning in a healthy, predictable, and personal regimen will set you up for increased productivity. Wake up early and rested. A must, is a good breakfast to fuel you, another key component is to partake in some form of physical activity — from a short vigorous workout to yoga, walking or simply focused breathing and stretching. You will find you become wakened and alert as a result — the lifelong benefits of regular exercise are immeasurable. Showering and taking time for personal grooming prepares you for the day. Also, reading inspiring or motivating information, quotes, or blogs, will set your mind to a strategic course. Finally, tackling something complex that requires your full attention will allow you a big accomplishment at the outset of your day. Your mind is active and ready to function in the morning.

You will notice I did not recommend reading the news, sleeping in, lounging around or reviewing your email. These habits will slow you down, fill your mind with negativity and distract you or force you to work on someone else's schedule. Your day will not move forward in a productive manner if you allow these behaviors to creep in to your daily routine.

The next key to daily productivity is something I call energy blocking. We all only have so much energy to focus on a project for any given amount of time. Some of us work well in 30 minute bursts; others can constructively sustain focus for up to 90 minutes. Whatever your focus zone is, you must understand this and work within it, taking healthy breaks of 10-15 minutes in between those periods. When I am working, I am notorious for taking frequent, short "walkabouts" for breaks. I liken it to coming up for air, then diving back down to work again. I am a pretty energetic guy and require these little releases of energy to maintain my productivity. I am very capable of working vigorously for long stretches, but when I am in that frame of mind, I ignore everything else, including food, hydration, and hygiene. Clearly that is not healthy, so I take my short walks and get back to work. These breaks will allow you to pause, restore, and refocus. For some it might be going for a walk around the block, for others, it might be making a personal call or doing a personal task. For others, it might simply be catching up on the day's events. You will find that moving through your day in this manner truly allows you to be more productive and more focused in the work you are doing. As I mentioned before, none of this will be possible unless you protect and schedule your time.

One important note; we all know that occasionally things

go haywire in our days. We must also accept that this might happen. While I strongly recommend a very structured approach to your days to maximize your productivity, it is also critical if, and when, things out of your control disrupt this, that you are able to refocus and get back on track without allowing such occurrences to create stress for you. It is not the action that disrupts you, it is your reaction to the disruption that needs to adapt. Developing a simple ritual to refocus is helpful. Think of an actor going through a dramatic and emotional scene. They might have to do twenty takes to get it just right. In between takes, when things go wrong, there are many distractions. There are make-up people, lighting, sound and other technicians working around them. There could be other actors creating challenges, there can be elements of the set that are distractions too, but a top quality actor will have very specific ways to center themselves and refocus. This might be breathing techniques, or mind clearing actions. It might include a verbal ritual or physical movement. They do this every time, then reset and begin their acting again. I recommend this simple technique. Take three minutes to do this and you'll be focused and ready to go after a disruption. Simply, stand (slowly) up out of your chair, placing one hand on your desk or chair for support as we do not want anyone falling over during this exercise. Close your eyes and breathe. Use a four count to breath in through you nose, hold for two counts, and then breathe out through your mouth for a five count. Doing this for two or three minutes will calm and center you. Open your eyes and get back to work.

WHAT IS YOUR CURRENT DAILY RITUAL?

DESCRIBE YOUR IDEAL DAILY RITUAL

PLAN YOUR PERFECT WORK DAY:

▶ MORNING RITUAL

▶ FOCUS TIME SEGMENTS

▶ RE-CHARGE/RE-FOCUS RITUAL

SECRET TIP 13

> " *limit,*
>
> *reduce, or*
>
> *outsource*
>
> *email handling* "

In the socially connected, yet non-verbal world of communications we are evolving into, there are very few ways to avoid email, text messages, instant messenger, or Twitter, etc. There are many extremely good things about using email. The obvious one is it helps us communicate directly with the recipient in a written context, and allows us to share documents and images efficiently. Another that I find extremely useful is that email is a powerful tool to use to provide scheduling and supporting information for live phone calls. It also helps expedite business driven requests that do not need the usual banter that phone communications bring. Remember, I schedule all my appointments and meetings and reviews, so when we need to simply communicate or confirm a recommendation or request that has a yes or no answer, it is a far more efficient use of time than a phone call. One thing we never do, though, is expect that the recipient will be "always" on and be at the ready to reply. If we want immediate confirmation, we simply make a direct call. Outside of the utilitarian use of email, there is an inordinate amount of junk and wasteful data flowing in every day.

I actually got to a point where I was simply reviewing email so it wouldn't pile up every day. Between 5pm at the end of every day and 6am the next day, my mailbox would amazingly fill up with no less than 150 emails. I always wondered why this occurred. I mean, most reasonable people or businesses wouldn't send, call you, or come to your office unannounced during those hours, so why should my inbox should be so stuffed during off hours? I'm not talking about the basic "flyers" that show up in my junk mail, I am talking about requests or comments or inquiries which actually are written in a manner that implies an immediate response is somehow expected. Are you kidding me? In order to keep my computer from crashing and inbox from exceeding its capacity, I needed to delete the email regularly. Typically, I would delete 140 emails, with ten being somewhat useful and when reviewing the ten, about seven of these were sent off and delegated to others, with three being left for me to deal with. While I became pretty efficient at dealing with this, it still was both time consuming and a daily ritual, in fact a compulsion, to log on and get to the email pile. If this had come in the form of a stack of mail, I know I would never have sifted through the pile. I would have allowed that stack to grow and grow. Determining what percentage of your email is important and what is junk is up to you. If you engage in reviewing your email first thing each day, you have already set your energy on a reactionary course, as opposed to a productive proactive one.

Responding to email places your time on "their" time. You are gradually drained of your freedom.

So what do you do? Well, you start by getting out of the habit of reviewing the first fifty emails of your day. They won't help you focus on the things that are important to you to achieve. Set a time to review them and delete the 90%+ of those emails that aren't important, and then set a time in your schedule to deal with the ones that might be important. Don't act on command ... be in demand! Responding like a dog to a dinner bell when the email arrives sets a precedent of expectation, turns your actions into reactions and distracts you from completion of important tasks in hand.

Another solution is to outsource this task or in-source it. Hire or assign someone to review your email. They can be an employee you already have, or you can actually outsource this. What is critical, to ensure that you do deal with the important communications that will be included in your email avalanche, is that you must take the upfront time to teach or train them to identify important information for you. Design a process to either have them bring the important stuff to your attention and use systems which can handle the processing and communications needs for this. I prefer scheduling time to deal with these things myself and in my investment business all my email must stay on the local server, so it cannot be outsourced. Some of the greatest marketing gurus of all time actually will go to the extent of having the email printed and review all of them on a specific day or specific times. Now I think that might be a colossal waste of paper, but paper is much more mobile, and easier to cart with you through airports, by the pool or other places...then be discarded. How you deal with this is up to you, but you must deal with it. If you even spent only an hour per day scrolling through your long list of email messages, you are losing an hour that could be spent, planning your next initiative, doing marketing, or furthering your sales.

DO YOU COMPULSIVELY
REVIEW AND RESPOND TO EMAILS?

DO YOU FEEL OVERWHELMED
OR CHAINED TO THIS HABIT?

MONITOR YOUR EMAIL FOR FIVE DAYS
AND UNCOVER WHAT YOU ARE REALLY RECEIVING.
IS IT NECESSARY OR IS IT WASTEFUL?

▶ CATEGORIZE YOUR EMAIL BY SENDER AND TOPIC

▶ RANK YOUR MAIL AS PRIORITY, TASK FOR LATER,
   OR GARBAGE

▶ SHARE THIS RANKING SYSTEM WITH THE
   PERSON WHO WILL REVIEW YOUR EMAIL AND
   COMMUNICATE A CLEAR STRATEGY FOR THIS
   PERSON TO BRING PRIORITY EMAIL TO YOUR
   ATTENTION.

SECRET TIP 14

"
use systems to leverage

your time and resources

to give you freedom
"

———————

"The amount of stress you feel in your life is in direct correlation to the lack of systems in your life."

– Davy Tyburski, COO, James Malinchak International.

Systems are applied to processes that make your business scalable.

They are everything ranging from simply using Outlook to hold contacts and manage email, to more complex CRM systems. Systems like Infusion Soft or A-Webber or Office Auto Pilot, will help you manage marketing and communication with your customers and prospects. There are systems for building things, tracking things, monitoring, etc. What is available for entrepreneurs includes technology and people. There are two things that must be done before you integrate systems into your life and business. The first, is to understand where your processes and business would be improved with better more efficient ways of doing things, second, you will need to hire or contract people who know how to maximize the use of such systems, so you can increase the time spent on marketing and sales. You will notice, that I did not recommend you learn how to use all these things yourself. Going back to our constant theme, you must be great at your core business and recognize where others can help. There are people who know how these things work, but you must identify what you might need, before you will find the right people.

Systems and software today are sophisticated tools. They allow you to learn about marketing your business as well. You can learn who is reading your information, how they found you, and where they go afterward. You can experiment with multiple marketing messages to determine which are the most effective.

Not many companies are leveraging technology to its fullest. There are many simple time and money saving solutions online. Something as simple as data entry can be outsourced through the internet inexpensively. By doing so, you are able to free up time for a staff member who can then focus on marketing or client facing activities — and in turn this creates funds or saves funds which you can then direct to hiring more staff to deal with customers or attract new ones.

Cloud technology is a major *disruptor* in on-line outsourcing and systems business. When working with a small business entrepreneur who ran an anti-snoring product company a colleague of mine learned the owner was having staff members enter data in multiple software programs, then reconciling it all manually. They were using QuickBooks, Google docs, Amazon for tracking orders, and another software program for tracking sales, and then taking time to combine all the information into usable data and statistics with minimal success. We investigated cloud applications which would take all that information in as it was realized and did the reconciliation all at once using the multiple streams of data. This completely freed up an enormous amount of time for her staff that were always busy in data entry. She decided that while she now had staff who had time on their hands, that she would not let them go, but train them to improve the sales and customer service side of her business. She was saving money on her employees' time and by re-directing her staff to revenue producing activities, increased her sales and profits. When your organization is not constrained by data entry or administrative tasks, the inputs become helpful outputs and you are able to focus on growing your business exponentially versus incrementally. Cloud technology is open and available in a lot of cases for free or a minimal investment. It also has the potential to allow businesses to scale like never before.

WHAT AREAS OF YOUR BUSINESS COULD BE DONE MORE EFFICIENTLY WITH THE USE OF BETTER SYSTEMS?

CAN YOU INVEST IN AN EXPERT IN SETTING UP SYSTEMS OR SIMPLY INTEGRATE EXISTING TECHNOLOGY INTO YOUR BUSINESS PROCESSES?

What are the leaders in your industry doing?

GET more freedom

SECRET TIP 15

" *seek points of leverage in marketing your business* "

If you work or serve customers directly in a business to consumer, "B2C", business, there are likely ways that you can tap business to business, "B2B", strategies to build your customer base. These strategies might be directly related to building a relationship with a business customer to access their many employees, or it can be through working with a credibility partner as I explained earlier in this book. Whichever business customer you identify, can leverage your reach and ability to get more sales as opposed to simply going after one-on-one sales. Strategic partnering and systems to support such activities can help you achieve the goal of building a reliable, repeatable pipeline of prospects or sales opportunities.

Leverage is most effective in marketing. Your overall reach is much bigger than you think.

One of my early coaching customers ran an online training enterprise. His customers were individuals who were upgrading or learning a specific type of project management software. His primary revenue stream was a membership model. He would use SEO and other online marketing tools, as well as an occasional classroom session to get the word out to individual users that he offered this training. This was a slow process that had a bit of traction and each was okay to build his membership. Once we were able to refine some processes and his marketing message, we were able to ramp his new member registrations up quite a bit, using his prospect pipelines, but we were not being as efficient as we could be. We had moved from three to six new members per month to eight to ten and higher, but we both agreed it would be much better if we could accelerate that, so we began to build marketing positioning for him to take on corporate RFPs. A successful RFP with the right corporate partner could mean up to three hundred employees signing up for online training at one time! We would blow his short term membership targets out of the water if we could simply engage the right single corporate partner. The leverage that would provide would be huge. He would continue marketing to individual customers, using all methods possible, but would add this new marketing leverage as well.

A corporate relationship is similar to a credibility partner. Successful engagement with these partners can provide your business scalable growth — however they can add risk if you become too reliant on the one relationship. The big opportunity is the leverage such a partner brings. To do this, you must enter the RFP process.

The effort to successfully apply, complete and submit a proposal in an RFP can be daunting. You often do not know who else is competing and how they are positioning their business case. A by-product of participating in this process is that it forces the entrepreneur to hone their marketing and positioning skills. You will sharpen your understanding of how you serve your individual customer. The benefits you bring as you position your offering to serve the larger business customer will become clearer. In my customer's case he became very clear on how what he offered the individual for online training became benefits for their employers. By doing so, he gained clarity on how to improve his offering to the individual. Learning the needs of the business finely tuned his marketing message to the single user. Ideally, the success of an RFP for my customer could see enormous growth result from a single effort; however the improvements to his marketing message for single users will also increase his memberships. With this newly uncovered knowledge he also began crafting a special report designed to highlight the greatest challenges and opportunities for employers seeking online training providers for their employees. He would do this to position himself as an important resource for companies in this situation. By doing so, he has gained leverage in positioning his marketing for the business customer. Where his competitors are clamouring to get access to RFP's, my customer is positioning himself to be sought out by them.

In my own experience, I have used the concept of leverage to further my own marketing efforts. My experience was in using credibility partners to extend my reach and gain leverage. Here's an example of this:

I decided to arrange a book signing a few years ago at a local Indigo book store and was thinking of ways to get the message out about the event. The intent was to spread the marketing message, which was used to build credibility for other initiatives I was undertaking about six weeks later. The idea was to remind people that I was the author of a book and that Indigo was hosting the event, thus increasing my credibility. I only had a few hundred contacts that I could send my information out to, so I worked to figure out how I could leverage my reach beyond my 300 or so contacts. Again, my primary goal was not to have a large audience at the event, it was to establish more credibility in the marketplace as an authority on the subject of philanthropy. I constructed a press release and an email letter to three key charities that I wished to support (that we had supported with my family foundation in the past). I offered to donate all profits from any sales on the book signing day to those charities and asked them if they would spread the word. They agreed. Before the event my marketing message went out to my 300 contacts and the three charities' other 3,000+ contacts! Ten times more! I ran a simple press release with a newswire service the day before the event and my reach expanded further. The book signing was on a sunny beautiful Saturday morning. Naturally, not many people showed up. Do you think I was concerned? No, not at all ... other than hoping to have sold books to give money to the charities. I was able to stay top of mind with my audience, I was able to capture images of me at the event in Indigo, with people lined up to buy my book, credible organizations promoted the event to their donors, and now my news release was parked on Google for years to follow. How can you leverage your contacts to help them and help you increase your reach?

WHERE ARE THE POINTS OF LEVERAGE FOR YOU IN MARKETING?

CAN YOU DIRECT YOUR ENERGY TO IDENTIFY ANOTHER SOURCE OF MARKETING WITH AN EXPONENTIAL OUTCOME?

WILL YOU INCLUDE A BUSINESS PARTNER OR A CREDIBILITY PARTNER IN THIS PROJECT?

SECRET TIP 16

" invest

for

growth

"

———————

Invest in experience and invest in knowledge — it is ALWAYS worth it.

I have had coaches and mentors all my life. I have had them in sports, in music, and business. There have been good coaches and not so good, but I have learned something from all of them. I would say the best teachers I have ever had have actually succeeded in some way in their field. Who do you believe would be the best to coach you? Someone who gets paid for what they are coaching, or someone who has never been paid? I have had coaches who hope to train me in building my investment business who never made a living at it. You might want to re-consider whether their advice will be helpful. That said, it is sometimes the case where they often stopped mid-way through whatever their profession was, though, to become a coach. They realized their unique ability and it drove them to coaching. They have hands-on experience and that's what gives them insight and allows them to relate. I have always participated at top levels in many areas and, in turn, I have been a coach in those areas, such as sports, education, financial planning, and business. My involvement as a coach or mentor has come from others asking for me to help them or share my experience and knowledge. I have now invested over $100,000 in the past five years in writing my books, travelling to and working with coaches, participating in mastermind groups and education. This is hard earned money that I have invested in furthering my knowledge and my own success. You can benefit from my investments and the investments of others who have gone before you. Coaching and advisory clients benefit from the knowledge I have gained and the investments I have made. I can comfortably say, that the return on my investment in me, has outstripped any investment I could have made in the stock market, or real estate during this period ... AND it has created the foundation for a lifetime of success and opportunity.

The time and wasted energy you save from learning from others who have gone before you is immeasurable. You gain freedom from doing it yourself and getting it wrong. The hours and dollars spent pursuing strategies and tactics which don't work are a heavy price to pay and they can also be emotionally draining. Entrepreneurs operate optimally when they are confident and energized, not demoralized by an ignorant or naïve mistake. There is no glory in learning from a school of hard knocks, when the collective wisdom of coaches and mentors can spare you a lot of the heartache. Coaches have even prevented me from doing damaging things to my business; they have streamlined processes for me and have shared wisdom that would have taken me years to learn on my own. The freedom I have gained from coaching is priceless.

Continue to invest in yourself. Invest every year in coaching and training. Invest the time and the people around you to receive coaching and training.

When you consider what you might invest in coaching or training, consider what the value of one customer or one idea is for you. You might find the three year value of one perfect customer is $30,000 to you. If that is the case, how much would you invest to attract that single customer? I know I'd invest up to $10,000 for that one customer because not only is that a solid return, but I would be able to replicate all I learned to attract more. If you could learn an idea that would save your business $30,000 of wasted time or investment what would that be worth to you? How about hiring the right person or people? What is that worth? It is important to understand the return on investment when you are considering working with a coach. If you invest money into a time saving process that teaches you how to grow quickly, and increase sales to your ideal customer, what ratio of investment to return is reasonable to you? Compare it to your investment return expectations or normal business growth expectations. Are you pleased with $1 invested and $1.50 returned ... or do you need $2? Within that process, you will establish the preferential financial leverage for you to make a commitment to coaching. The intangible upside can even be more valuable.

WHO ARE YOUR COACHES AND MENTORS RIGHT NOW?

WHAT IS THE DOLLAR VALUE OF YOUR IDEAL CUSTOMER?
ONE YEAR AND THREE YEAR VALUE TO YOUR BUSINESS.

WHAT IS THE ONE THING YOU HOPE TO LEARN
THAT MIGHT INCREASE YOUR REVENUE
OR SAVE YOU TIME AND MONEY RIGHT NOW?

GET more freedom

SECRET TIP 17

" unplug

the

drain "

Do you have that one person (there are likely more than one) in your life, work or personal, who constantly complains about their circumstances? You know that one person who has drama all the time. You find yourself drawn into their chaos somehow and become distracted or pulled down with them for a moment. Their lives are stuck in a never ending pattern of conflict or complaint — they are like a "floater" that just won't be flushed. Sometimes they are friends in your network who generally are likeable and have been in your life for a while. You have always accepted their drama with a grain of salt.

Well, life is too short and your time is too precious to allow others to hold you back or drain your energy.

So many people benefit from you when you are energized and positive. Therefore, today is the day to retake your energy and allow the "drainers" to swirl in the bowl and disappear. These are people who are in your life — personal and work life — who suck the life right out of you. They are the constant complainers and the "Wendy Whiners" (thank you SNL). You ask them how they're doing and their drama begins, and then ends an hour later. They want to pull you into their misery. Their negativity draws you in. A simple solution is to pull the plug and allow them to swirl about the drain, disappearing out of your life. This does not have to be done harshly or hastily. You can simply reduce the time you spend with them progressively and don't engage them in their misery. Eventually they will stop connecting because they can't suck any energy out of you. They will move on to someone who they can.

Remove the drama and the time wasters from your life. Replace your drainers by adding or including only those people who energize you and want the best for you. This will enhance your life and bring your energy up. Your creativity will soar when you share your thoughts and time with people who are positive and share your passions for success.

"Great minds discuss ideas. Average minds discuss events. Small minds discuss people."

— Eleanor Roosevelt

WHO ARE THE DRAINERS IN YOUR LIFE RIGHT NOW?

LIST THEM BY NAME.

WHO ARE THE PEOPLE WHO LIFT YOU UP AND ENERGIZE YOU?

LIST THEM BY NAME.

SECRET TIP 18

" dump

the

meetings "

AVOID at all costs, unnecessary meetings. They are the biggest waste of time — EVER! I have yet to be in a meeting where the result is accomplishment. I will be the first to admit, that the longer I sit in a meeting, the more and more aggravated I get. I spend my time in those meetings thinking of all the more productive things I could be doing while I tune out the uninspiring conversation. For me, the best thing to reduce my own irritation would be to never attend.

There is nothing so important to be discussed in a meeting that you will need to be there.

If it is that important, there will be someone who can provide you the "Coles notes" version — or a memo that summarizes the main points. You can review and absorb this information at your own pace/schedule ... AFTER you have accomplished something that is important to you. Even taking a walk to clear your head and refresh is better than time spent wasted in a meaningless meeting. Attending a meeting is not a break.

I like to set up customer facing appointments or calls during the exact time of a meeting so I can make productive use of my time and not be questioned. It is an easy way to gently decline any meeting. Sometimes, I simply close my office door and carry on working with no explanation at all.

As for you, don't call meetings. They are simply a platform for you or someone else to project your idea of what is important onto people who do not share that opinion. Send a memo, email, or have a scheduled, short one on one meeting (or small group) to get your point across and end the meeting. It is not a forum for gripes or concerns. If you must hold or attend a meeting, do not ask or encourage questions that are not specific to the topic at hand. Have an agenda, hand it out well ahead of the meeting and stick to the agenda. Set expectations, demand accountability, and increase communication ... but don't waste everyone's time with meetings.

How many meetings do you attend
in a two week period?

What constructive methods will you use to avoid
attending meetings in the future?

GET more freedom

SECRET TIP 19

" don't serve
the wrong
customer "

———•———

Accepting customers, who do not fit your ideal customer profile; will only lead to future stress. It might seem reasonable that you get a short term sale and add another possible contact and referral source, but if they are not a fit, there is a strong possibility they sure will cost you in the long run. They might not even cost you directly, in terms of money, but they will cost you in stress or time. They will suck the time and energy from you and your support staff. They will corner you to do more of what is unproductive and time wasting than you should. They will pull you outside your unique ability and distract you from bigger things. The wrong customer is like a disease. They will eat away at your productivity and your energy. You cannot allow this to happen. In the financial service industry (no different than the insurance, legal, accounting, real estate, or most other service based industries) we were taught early on in our careers that anyone with a pulse and a pocketbook are a potential client. When you are starting out, you only focus on growth, as fast as possible, so you can increase your revenue, pay your bills and gain acceptance with your managers and your peers. Build your numbers and the revenue will come. And you know what? It is true. The numbers do come ... your revenue grows, your customer list grows and so do your headaches. At one time, early on in my career in the nineties, I worked with a senior partner and the two of us had over 1,200 investment clients! It was insane. We had six phone lines going off constantly. Email was not really established yet, but I can only imagine what kind of avalanche that would have been. There was absolutely no planning for the future or any staffing or systems in place. It was impossible! We were just running as fast as we could to keep up with the influx of demand. When things went poorly, inevitably, we lost a lot of clients ... which we had to go out and replace. It was a horrendous treadmill we were on for three years and when I jumped off, I vowed never to jump back on.

When you work with the wrong clients, they assume their pleasure or challenges will be your only focus. They don't respect your time and they don't respect your value.

Understand this is NOT their fault. You are the one who determines who you let in and how you will serve them. In my investment business and coaching I have raised the bar very high on the commitment I ask of my new clients. By design, the hurdle has kept a lot of people from working with me and sometimes it is tempting to be more flexible. However, on the positive side, I engage fewer families, but they are more committed, more enjoyable, and have a strong understanding of the value I provide them. Today, less than 75 client families make up all of our investment management households. In my coaching business I will only accept an ongoing 25 ideal candidates per year.

When putting up barriers to filter out the wrong clients, you need to get comfortable with the phrase "It's not for everyone". It must become part of your vocabulary. Placing the onus on the prospect to achieve a higher standing to become a customer either repels them or attracts them to you. Either way you both win. Wrong fit customers are not an opportunity for you to change their behaviors or mindset, they will drain you. Remember, "It's not for everyone". This mantra will free you.

Not accepting the wrong customer is one thing, the next is to constructively dismiss the people you are working with today who are not an ideal customer. This will be a relief for both you and them. These are typically people who you have already "quiet filed". The relationship has been over for a while, yet neither of you wants to take the next step to end it. Make a plan and set the date, then end those relationships.

The result of no longer working with the wrong customer, is that you look forward to everyone you do work with who are right for your business. You will be energized and your time will be respected. Your employees will happily service your ideal customers and everyone will benefit. Freedom is achieved when you are of service and respected for it.

LIST YOUR TOP FIVE WRONG FIT CUSTOMERS.

POST A WRITTEN DESCRIPTION
OF YOUR IDEAL CUSTOMER PROFILE NEAR YOUR DESK
AND REVIEW IT EVERY TIME YOU CONSIDER
ACCEPTING SOMEONE WHO IS NOT THE RIGHT CUSTOMER

GIVE back

to your community

and the causes

that matter most to you

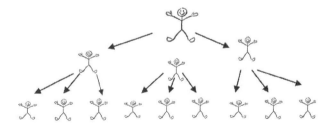

I had a client, Dan, who had amassed a considerable amount of wealth through his various businesses in his lifetime. We would meet once a year for a coffee to review his investments and financial picture. One Friday not many years ago, we were sitting at this café with our various papers laid on the table, and our coffee cups placed on top of them. As always, our conversation focused on the Calgary Flames and a variety of topical news stories of the day. In a break of tradition, Dan spoke up and told me he was concerned that he hadn't planned on whom to leave his wealth to. I was a bit surprised at the change in topic, but engaged him and asked what he meant.

"Well," he continued, "as you know, my wife passed a few years ago and my children are living successful lives with their own families. I am proud of their accomplishments and they are independently wealthy. They don't need my money." I prompted him forward. "Yes, I know this." He continued, "It is just that in my 84 years, I haven't ever really considered how I might pass on any kind of legacy beyond my family. There is a lot of money to consider and I want it to have the biggest impact. As well, I'd rather not give to the government either if possible."

Naturally I was really beginning to wonder where this was headed. We hadn't gotten into these things in the past, as Dan was a pretty private person. So I asked him, "Dan, this is not our usual chit chat. Why has this become so important to you?" Dan replied, "I saw my doctor last month to go through a battery of tests. I hadn't been feeling very well and I was hoping to learn why. Well, the reason was that I have been diagnosed with pancreatic cancer and it is spreading. My doctor says I only have weeks to live."

It was as though I'd been hit by a truck. The shock to hear such a thing from a wonderful man and good friend was too much. I had a hard time expressing my emotions, so I simply moved to my advisor mode and asked him if he wanted to come by my office on Monday morning and we could begin working on some planning and maybe sort things out for him quickly. He agreed.

Monday came and I had blocked a few hours (no calls, no interruptions) in the morning for our discussion. I was well prepared, had done a lot of research and reviewed what I knew of his financial circumstances. I am not entirely sure what I was thinking when we started the meeting. I somehow had a grand idea of Dan working through all his issues over the weekend and showing up with a plan. Well, that couldn't be further from the truth. Dan was not any clearer on things than he was when we met Friday. So we began, from scratch. The first meeting didn't get us very far, but it was a start. We pre-scheduled meetings for the next two Mondays. The next Monday, Dan had to cancel. He had been to the hospital over the weekend. The following week he cancelled as well. The cancer had taken a hold of him and he passed away just three weeks from our coffee meeting. I was shaken and upset. I had lost a friend, the world lost a great man and he was not able to express his true giving nature before he left this world. When I heard the following Oliver Wendell Holmes quote I was reminded of him, "Alas for those who never sing, but die with all their music in them."

If anything, our lives are dreadfully short. We move through life trying to do our best to live well and with prosperity. Some of us accomplish a lot in business and become wealthy and successful. This is hard work and for most, it is all consuming. Sometimes our families take a back seat, and a lot of times we barely impact the world around us and our communities the way we had hoped. But when all the effort is expended on our business, and we have aged a bit and we look back on our lives and accomplishments, it is normal to want to give back. In a lot of cases, some of the possibilities to have the biggest impact have slipped away, like with Dan. There are tools or strategies that just don't work at their age or circumstance. They can still do something, but maybe not quite with the potential impact as at a younger age.

You are reading this because you want to learn to grow your business and get more freedom to enjoy your life and family even more, but you also have a sense of commitment to a bigger impact. You know as well as I do, that we go around once and if we want to do great things, we must start today. In this next segment I will help you connect with your philanthropic side and teach how to implement strategies that will help you enjoy big impact giving.

SECRET TIP 1

" connect

passion

with purpose "

———•———

When building your "tribe" you will find people who not only buy your products or services, but share your values. In fact, when your passion is clear and your purpose is understood by everyone around you, they will be attracted to you. Stay focused on this. It is your compass; never change your "due North" setting.

Whenever you are lost, come back to the passions that guide you and the purpose which drives you.

Earlier I spoke of moving forward with passion in your business, but simply being passionate about something is not enough. Sharing an ideal with people, customers, and partners is a start, but to what end? There is a need to put passion behind purpose and then push forward to achieve your vision or goals. Victor Frankl described in his bestselling book, "Man's Search for Meaning", a harrowing recollection of his survival in the Nazi concentration camps during the Holocaust. He made important observations as to why some people survived and others simply did not. Beyond the randomness of the indiscriminate killings, each day, week, month, and year, there was a gruelling battle for survival. Some people succumbed and died, others survived. Frankl survived and summarized that it was his will to survive that came from his life's purpose. He had a strong commitment to a personal and immensely important purpose and goal on which to focus upon. The first was to be with his beloved wife and family again, the next to share with and teach the world his observations about purposeful existence and survival. In his words, describing the meaning of life, he said, "Everyone has his own vocation or mission in life to carry out a concrete assignment which demands fulfillment. Therein he cannot be replaced, nor can his life be repeated ..."

While obviously far removed from the gravity of the life or death struggle faced by Frankl, connecting your passion with your actual purpose moves your life and your business to an important end result. A purposeful existence drives us daily to have an impact. It allows us to reach for a higher goal. Your purpose is not required to carry the weight of a concentration camp existence on its shoulders; however, it should hold you up in times of great stress and give you direction when you need a compass. A life without purpose is an empty life.

People and customers who share this with you will want to become part of your efforts to make a difference. Share your vision with them openly and often. Start by identifying your purpose and describing your passion to achieve your goals.

WHAT IS YOUR PURPOSE?

DESCRIBE YOUR PASSION IN DETAIL

▷ START WITH, "I HAVE GREAT PASSION FOR WHAT I DO, BECAUSE ..."

SECRET TIP 2

" connect to a cause

through

your experience "

Connecting your purpose and future actions to a larger cause will build a bigger goal to move you forward. It will help you identify with your community. Making this known as part of your overall mission, or connection to your business will help you to attract customers who share the same ideals and goals. It is important to both you and your ideal customer. In a way, it will bind you in a common effort knowing that their connection to you and your business will help them achieve their own personal goals to give back.

By helping to support a cause they care about you continue to serve your customers.

It is your decision whether you choose to support multiple causes or a single one as you define your giving strategy. This will be clear to you when you review your life experiences and identify those which changed the course of your life and were integral in forming you and your outlook on the world. There could be numerous things which matter to you that you feel a connection with. I have written about this in my two prior books on philanthropy and found in my research that every major philanthropist connects their most important efforts to support causes which they were directly affected by in some way in their lives. It might be extremely specific, like finding a cure or treatment for throat cancer or more general, such as supporting research for all forms of cancer. Whichever it is, the deep rooted connection is personal. It might be a result of something, good or bad, that happened to them. It could have also been and event they witnessed or something that occurred to someone else.

For me, a life experience that has centered my focus was growing up in a poor neighborhood where my peer group of friends did not experience the same life opportunities I did because of the love and support I received from my parents. In my life I have experienced advantages that some have not, while some of my neighbourhood friends were lost from the day they were born. Naturally, as I look around today, none of those kids have grown up in my peer group. They never had a chance to succeed like I have. In 2008, I established the Fit Family Fund to provide financial support for our key pillars of family support: 1. funding family physical health and nutrition, 2. funding for education, 3. funding for protection of children. An additional goal of this was to help bring my family closer to a singular effort to help other families realize the opportunities I had. Each year, we gather to review our three pillars and make decisions about giving based on the charities that we have learned do the most to make an impact in those areas.

Through my twenty years in the financial profession, I have been given an expertise that allows me to do more on a collective basis than what I could achieve on my own. When I feel bothered in my day to day business, or irritated by someone or something which distracts my attention from our core business, instead of letting it get to me, I reflect on my purpose to help others re-direct as much money and energy back to charitable causes as I possibly can. It is way easier to work through challenging days when my larger goal is something that will make a big impact.

WHAT LIFE EXPERIENCES SHAPED YOUR VIEWS?

WHAT "CAUSE" WILL THIS RELATE TO FOR YOU?

SECRET TIP 3

" select

an organization(s)

to support "

Once you're motivated to help and prepared to take real action, you have to stop and think about whom you want to help, how you want to help and exactly what you want the results to be. I have identified three key steps to making a big impact through giving that I'll share with you.

The first is to always pick the cause with which you connect on the most profound level. In order to commit to make long term difference, you need to find something that really speaks to you to be sure you'll give it the utmost care and attention. Ask yourself, "*If I were able to make a difference for this cause, what would that look like? What would an organization have to do to help me achieve my philanthropic goals? What are their values? Are they effective?*"

How do you find a charity that fits your cause of choice? Leverage the internet's search engines by plugging in the relevant search terms, and then take the time to sift through the organizations and websites that pop up. Remember that building an attractive, user-friendly website that sums up that charity's core message in a few paragraphs and pages is unimaginably easier than actually building and running an effective charity that consistently delivers measurable results to the cause in question. Look closely at a big philanthropic organization and you will see that it is much like a big business. It might be incredibly well run, but that's not a given, which is why you must execute due diligence before you hand over a dime.

Let's look at homelessness as an example and start with the big picture. If you decide that you want to "end homelessness", you need to recognize that this is a real stretch goal. It's huge and far-reaching because homelessness exists on both a local and global level.

Let's narrow it down. Do you want to tackle homelessness in your own city? Do you want to reach across the country or around the world? Is putting a roof over a family's heads enough or do you want to address the root cause of their homelessness? Do you focus on those who are homeless right now or do you figure out how to keep the next generation from being homeless?

If you decide that affordable housing is the key, you may immediately think of Habitat for Humanity. A well-recognized brand that's lauded for the work it does, Habitat for Humanity may be a good fit but you may also decide that you could provide a "fresh approach and perspective", or "strategies and actions".

Time and again, I've seen budding philanthropists with a deep commitment and raging passion decide that they could produce better results if they started from scratch and created a new organization. While I'd never warn you entirely against launching your own charity, I will point out that you really need to understand the philanthropic landscape and that founding and operating a charity can be even more challenging than running your own company.

As a charity, financial accountability is a major issue and impeccable financial reporting must be a given if you want to maintain your charitable status. Are you really interested in acquiring both the philanthropic and financial expertise required to run your new charity? Can you accept and deal with the fact your actions, personal and professional, will likely be subject to intense public and media scrutiny whether or not they have anything to do with your charity?

Attracting and raising the capital needed to develop and fund the necessary infrastructure and/or grow the organization requires a different approach. As well, it is invariably a much harder pitch when investors will see social and other intangible benefits, such as a sense of wellbeing, instead of monetary returns.

You should start by asking yourself certain tough questions. *"Why do I think I can do a better job than existing charities? Why do I really want to start my own charity? Will my charity actually achieve better results? What is the real cost of creating a redundant organization to the cause? Is this about my need for control and/or recognition?"*

In Canada alone, there are approximately 86,000 registered charities, so I truly believe that if you look, you will find one that is as committed to your cause as you are.

The second secret to making a big impact through giving is to always choose a charity that takes the action(s) required to produce sustainable results for the cause you want to impact.

Should you decide to work with an existing philanthropic organization, you want to be sure it supports the very goals that are important to you, but as importantly you need tangible proof that they take the actions required to produce the specified results. If you wanted to help reduce or eliminate homeless in Calgary or a city like it, what would you do? How would you choose to help?

While your ultimate focus might be homelessness, you may want to step back to address one of its root causes to prevent rather than address homelessness after the fact. For instance, if someone you know ended up on the street due to poverty resulting from a combination of addictions and mental health issues such as depression or severe anxiety disorder, you could help an organization that supports people with addictions and mental health issues.

My third and final secret to making a big impact through giving is to always invest the time and effort required to thoroughly research and assess the charity that you have identified as the one that takes the actions required to produce sustainable results for the cause you want to support.

Once you've found the organization and determined that it takes the actions that deliver the results, you're ready for the next steps. Do you feel good about that charity?

Don't answer that question until you can show me that you've done your due diligence.

Committing to any charity before checking it out is at best naïve, and at worst, irresponsible.

It could be akin to pitching your money out the proverbial window.

You'll need to consider and assess their management team, infrastructure, fundraising costs versus funds raised, financial reporting and status, tangible, measurable results and much more.

NAME THE CAUSE OR CAUSES
YOU FEEL MOST CONNECTED TO:

WHAT CHARITIES HAVE YOU IDENTIFIED TAKE ACTION
TO ENSURE THE SUSTAINABILITY OF THEIR IMPACT?

CREATE YOUR OWN CHARITY
DUE DILIGENCE CHECKLIST:

- WHAT DOES THE CHARITY DO?

- WHO ARE THE BENEFICIARIES?

- IS THE CHARITY MAKING AN IMPACT?

- DO THEY DIRECT THE RIGHT AMOUNT OF FUNDS (65% OR MORE) DIRECTLY ON THEIR BENEFICIARIES?

- ARE THEY SUSTAINABLE?

- CAN THEY ARTICULATE A CLEAR PLAN FOR SUCCESS?

SECRET TIP 4

"
decide
to do
something
"

Seems simple, yet mentally projecting your positive energy through a decision isn't going to accomplish much. In this case, "decision" is an action. Almost 30 years ago, Nike launched their "Just Do It" campaign and it immediately became synonymous with success and action. Deciding to do something commits you to big impact giving. The very first step is identifying what your life experiences were and how you will connect this to action. You will need to identify which cause(s) you will support, and then you must review how you might become involved. Either you will support charities which serve the cause, or you might even begin your own charity or foundation to have a more direct impact. There are so many deserving charities which exist and would make tremendous use of what you have to give. You'll find doing more homework to uncover them might be more rewarding than starting something from scratch.

The most important step is to take action. By identifying what you bring to the table with your own strengths you will learn how you will have the biggest impact. You will be giving with time, money, and influence.

Once you understand what your greatest strength is you can learn how to give.

We give money in obvious ways through straight financial donations, but we can also give money in more strategic ways. Investing in areas which clear the way or enable your charity to execute their mission more effectively is one way. Providing goods or services is another. For example, a home builder who wishes to help provide affordable housing could offer supplies or labor to Habitat for Humanity in their efforts to construct new homes.

We give our time in so many ways, from coaching kids' sports, to volunteering at the local food bank. Filling a needed and important volunteer role brings us closer to the cause and often the beneficiaries of our efforts. Another way volunteering can have a big impact is through participation on committees or boards of directors and even in outside advisor roles. This type of volunteerism can be a tremendous way to connect your specific skills with impactful giving.

Lastly, there is the gift of influence. This is realized largely through advocacy. Our role in the community as entrepreneurs, business people, and community leaders offers us a platform to vocalize our commitment to a cause(s) and encourage others to join our efforts. During interviews for my very first book, "Philanthropy; An Inspired Process", one of Calgary's most identifiable philanthropists graciously invested his time with me to share his thoughts and own experiences of giving. One of his most important contributions had been the establishment of a cardiovascular research center which had ostensibly created treatments for heart disease and unquestionably saved the lives of hundreds of patients. This was something I was certain he would claim as one of his most important rewards in giving — and I am certain it was — but when asked what his greatest enjoyment in philanthropy was, he stated it was influencing his wealthy (or wealthier) friends to write larger and larger cheques to fund the charities he supported. One of his greatest strengths in giving was his ability to attract more and more funding to a cause in need. He was clear on where he would have the biggest impact and in ways that was through his ability to influence others.

I have written about how philanthropy can be defined as the "love of mankind". Well that love is beautiful, but if you simply exist to enjoy the feeling, then not much gets accomplished, does it? It is the decision to act that does. Moving your philanthropy from your personal experience and an idea to action requires motivation. Make the decision to move forward.

WHAT WILL YOU GIVE?

- TIME?

- MONEY?

- INFLUENCE?

GIVE back

SECRET TIP 5

" devise

a strategy to give

which plays

into your strengths

"

Previously I mentioned that the first steps in your journey to give back, are to bring your personal experiences and motivations to the table and then see how the cause which you wish to support might connect to your business and your customers. In my two books on the subject of philanthropy and the previous segment, I revealed that taking the time to know how a cause is served by a charity, matters. Solving homelessness happens in a variety of ways. It can be through building homes (i.e. Habitat for Humanity), or subsidizing rents, or through employment creation initiatives, or family services. You must decide which cause is sensible for you to fund and align with an organization that is best suited to make an impact.

Let's look at what you might be able to do as an entrepreneur. Let's say your business is in the homebuilding industry and you have identified that the cause you wish to support is fighting homelessness. When you did your research, you found that among the many solutions that are out there for this cause, it was the construction of a home which gave new owners a sense of pride and belonging. The new homeowner instantly became more connected with their community and confident in their place in the world. This translated to better behaviors and achievement in other areas, such as their employment and education of their children. In order to develop your giving strategy, you identified that your company had excess materials and reduced pricing for materials due to your relationship with suppliers. For a reasonable investment and productive use of your overstock you could provide Habitat for Humanity with enough building materials to complete three homes. As a result you launched a public awareness campaign through your company that rewards your customers by connecting them to giving success simply by selecting your organization over others. A portion of your profits would be used to fund materials, while the simple act of building a home created "leftovers" that were also donated. By making this a corporate initiative, you attract more like minded customers and do more to further your goals to make an impact.

Another example, could be how the homebuilders who constructed our home in 2006, have been giving back to the community and directing their efforts to cancer research by offering up their show homes each year to the various home lottery campaigns to raise funds for Alberta's two main cancer charities. This initiative generates tens of thousands of dollars for the charities and provides a strong connection for the company to their own desired giving goals. Additionally, as people become aware of the home that is being given away, more and more people will choose to view the home. This will provide an incredible experiential marketing opportunity for the builder to showcase their craft to new potential buyers.

How you build your strategy to give back that incorporates your personal and/or business strengths, is up to you. I urge you to

consider innovative and effective ways that bring the most impact to the cause,

that help you and your customers connect in a manner that is collaborative with a shared purpose and also in a way which can contribute to your bottom line — naturally allowing you to have more and more impact over time.

If you choose to make a personal contribution, you will need to review the same general principles of selecting the cause and the organization that will help before you invest your own resources for impact. You can give anonymously or openly, it is up to you. I prefer disclosing philanthropy in order to be a role model and an agent of influence in giving. In my own view, sharing your philanthropy in a public manner is not with the intent to gain public acceptance or accolades, but as a way to lead others by example. As a corporate leader you can extend your social leadership through sharing.

Another important consideration for giving personally is to seek out guidance from specialists in the area of planned giving. These individuals might be your financial advisors, or they could be your accountant, lawyer, or a planned giving professional working with a charity. For precisely the same reasons customers seek you out for your specialized products or services, you too should seek the strategic counsel of professionals who are experts in planned giving. By working with the right person you will be astounded at the possibilities for impact they uncover for you, and that you never knew you had.

WHAT ASPECTS OF YOUR BUSINESS
ARE CONNECTED TO YOUR CAUSE?

HOW WILL YOU LEVERAGE THIS TO HAVE A BIG IMPACT?

HOW CAN YOU ENGAGE YOUR CUSTOMERS
TO SUPPORT YOU, OR EVEN TO PROMOTE YOUR CAUSE
TO ATTRACT MORE CUSTOMERS?

SECRET TIP 6

" know

what you bring

to the table

"

In the first section of this book I encouraged you to identify your unique ability and strengths in order to grow a strong and profitable niche business. It is those attributes you should leverage when deciding how you can make a big impact. Understanding what you bring to the table is important. You might find you are better at making strategic decisions. You might mobilize and influence people better than most, or maybe directing financial resources is what you do. Or is your biggest asset business building? Whatever the case might be, you should investigate this for yourself. Simply because you are passionate about a cause and have a strong desire to experience your impact firsthand, doesn't mean you would be best suited or most impactful to serve food at the homeless shelter. Maybe your big impact giving would be better realized by using your contacts to help source or transport the food that will be served daily.

As in any successful business, you need to ask yourself how you or your organization will create leverage. If you are going to step up and bring a non-profit social enterprise to life, how would you help it to grow and thrive the same as you would in a for-profit setting? There have been many companies over the years which have added unique social enterprise to their for-profit offering. From Starbucks and their Fair Trade Certified™ coffee, to CIBC Run for the Cure's ongoing support for the Canadian Breast Cancer Foundation, or even when the show Survivor auctions off its props from each season to raise funds for the Elisabeth Glaser Pediatric AIDS Foundation, etc.

The more entrepreneurs acknowledging their strongest attributes, the more unique and creative ways social enterprise will evolve.

WHAT DO YOU BRING TO THE CAUSE?

- ARE YOU STRATEGIC?

- ARE YOU A CONNECTOR?

- ARE YOU A FINANCIAL EXPERT?

- IS GOVERNANCE YOUR THING?

- WHAT OTHER QUALITIES AND SKILLS CAN

  YOU OFFER?

GIVE back

SECRET TIP 7

" *redefine*

giving

"

While there are a multitude of organizations doing so many different things, fundamentally their causes remain pretty much the same. Caring for and protecting animals is a fairly constant theme or cause. Achieving impact, though, can occur in a variety of ways. Traditional approaches are rescue or providing homes for animals, but innovative methods have been applied to screening and progressions for families adopting pets. Community outreach and advocacy of animal care and welfare are preventative measures that reduce abuse or neglect. Not all methods will be or should be conventional. One organization in Calgary has a multi-step animal adoption process, where the initial introduction is made at the kennel. The next is an interview process, then a brief introduction at the family's home, then approval and a gradual move to make it a permanent home and adoption.

> You are an innovator in business, extend that for your big impact giving by becoming an innovator in social good.

There are so many ways entrepreneurs can change the way we give. They are doing it all the time. Everything from micro-loan programs to work share to social enterprise requires innovative thinking. My new and remarkable friends Craig and Marc Kielburger redefined giving with an entrepreneurial spirit and vision that has created the inspiring We Day phenomenon to bring attention and support to their **Free the Children** charity. They believe *"in a world where all children are free to achieve their fullest potential as agents of change."* Their mission is *"to empower youth to remove barriers that prevent them from being active local and global citizens."* The Kielburgers understood the power of influencing change through grassroots levels — adolescents. The energy that children bring combined with the future influence they will have, gives their We Day events its power as it is used to reward teens for giving back. We Day are events held in cities across North America and the United Kingdom. The We Day events are now a major draw across North America, attracting some of the most important key note speakers of our time such as Martin Luther King Junior III, Magic Johnson, Mikhail Gorbachev, Larry King — and some of the most exciting contemporary music acts, such as Nelly Furtado, Hedley, Down With Webster, and Macklemore — for free. Major corporations have realized the potential and now are providing significant funding for the events. The Kielburgers' vision and entrepreneurial spirit has redefined the way teens are moved to connect with charity. They raise funds for Free the Children and We Day from individuals, and over the years, they have attracted a substantial amount of sponsorship from major corporations who understand the impact We Day has. Major companies, such as Royal Bank of Canada (RBC), Potash Corp., Allstate, Microsoft, Virgin Atlantic, and Barclays to name a few, have made considerable financial commitments. Their Free the Children charity raised over $40 million worldwide in 2013 while a couple hundred thousand screaming and cheering teen ambassadors across the continent are now carrying the We Day message to their peers, their communities, and home to their parents. The Kielburgers have combined traditional charity work, social enterprise, social networks, grassroots programs, volunteerism, and a strong celebrity connection to change the way giving back is implemented. They have made global impact cool among the toughest demographic to inspire. Their platform is unique and they've turned giving on its head.

Now you don't have to emulate Craig and Marc in your efforts to have a big impact. However, you are a leader in your market for a reason ... most likely because you had a unique vision for opportunity that no one else quite did. Challenge your innovative side to find the connection between your vision and really making change.

WHAT INNOVATIVE IDEAS DO YOU HAVE THAT WILL HELP
TO EXECUTE YOUR BIG IMPACT GIVING?

How does your unique business positioning give you an innovative edge?

SECRET TIP 8

" *serve*

    others

"

Serve your customer by connecting with their desires to contribute or give back. Give to your customers in many ways by supporting the causes they care about, by sponsoring them or an event they are close to. You might even be able to use your platform to bring awareness to causes that matter to them. You have a moral responsibility to learn about them and what their needs are, then provide them with the best suited strategy and solutions that you have to offer them.

By engaging their personal views and goals, you are able to connect more deeply with them.

Serve your community by recognizing the position you have in your community and give back. Your early entrepreneurial successes are derived from the community you live and work in. As a citizen it is important that you become aware of the opportunities you might provide others. By giving back to the community, you are opening doors for others. The collective success of a healthy and strong community builds better businesses, better families, and a stronger economic climate.

Serve your family. This is an extremely important aspect of giving back. It is not charitable in the conventional sense, but building stronger caring families is key to developing stronger communities. Pay attention to your personal relationships by serving your family. There is nothing more precious in our lives.

Make time for yourself by making time for travel. Expanding

your mind through global experiences helps to center us. We all learn from our experiences in travel that people all over have similar basic needs, yet also have very different lives, opportunities, or stresses. Understanding how you fit in a global sense will help you gain perspective on what you have and what others might not.

When you deal with your friends and family, be present. Take yourself away from your work and your planning, and focus on the people you are with. I heard a funny joke by a comedienne once about her husband's marriage proposal. She was so happy to get his attention for a moment while he proposed. She joked he *"muted the TV — ok, the game — at half time — to ask the question"*. While humorous and maybe a bit unlikely, the point was clear. Everyone laughed because we can all relate to this in some way. Our lives are full of distractions and we must work very hard to block those out when dealing with our family or friends in the moment. My parents often say that my wife, I, and our kids travel a lot. They are right. We don't do too many large longer trips, but we get away frequently for extra-long weekends. I have found over the years, the best way to focus solely on our family and limit the distractions of work is to remove ourselves completely from our daily routines. Going away allows us this opportunity. In a sense, we plug in to each other, while unplugging from our distracting lives.

What we admittedly need to do more of and have begun to do, is to explore. Travelling to new places, and experiencing new cultures and lifestyles is part of our ongoing travel plans. The education for our children is amazing and the shared experience is good for all of us.

HOW WILL YOU SERVE YOUR CUSTOMERS BETTER?

- WHAT WILL YOU DO?

- WHEN WILL YOU START?

HOW WILL YOU SERVE YOUR COMMUNITY?

- WHAT WILL YOU DO?

- WHEN WILL YOU BEGIN?

HOW WILL YOU SERVE YOUR COMMUNITY?

- WHAT WILL YOU DO?

- WHEN WILL YOU BEGIN?

SECRET TIP 9

" pre–serve

yourself

"

Preserving your mental health is an important way to serve yourself.

Give yourself permission to take time for you.

This is a hard thing to do for the wired entrepreneur. This means changing your hard driving mindset focused on always moving forward, to allow for time *away* from work. From 2005 through 2011, I was training very heavily for a variety of triathlon races. My longest was a half ironman, or a 70.3 event. It is a five and a half hour event (for me). The training for a triathlon can be immensely taxing at times — from both a physical point of view and a mental one — even more specifically, a time management one. If you want to perform well and not drop out due to exhaustion, you must "put in the miles" or you'll be very painfully surprised by your body's reactions late in the event. I learned mid-way through those years that putting in no miles is better than putting in bad ones. While you are constantly compelled to squeeze your workouts in, it is sometimes more important to take time away to recover, to rejuvenate, rest, and repair. As you age, it becomes even more important to listen to your body for this. The same is true in the business world. It is impossible to be effective and keep your foot to the pedal constantly. Without a doubt something will break down. Taking time for yourself on regular intervals will help to extend your run. Additionally, knowing when those "bad mile days" are happening is important. When they occur, you have to give yourself permission to simply step away and regroup without guilt. You'll be better for it.

You can help pre-serve yourself, by setting personal goals. It is simple. When you write down the business goals that are most important to you, they tend to happen. When you write down personal goals that you wish to have in your life that are NOT work related, they also tend to happen more, as opposed to never doing it. Time will escape you and life will throw curves, so if you haven't written down your own personal goals and taken steps to achieve them, you will find they are pushed aside. Put them on paper and plan for them. Next, share them with someone you trust. That added level of accountability helps.

Take care of your personal health. There is nothing more important in this world than our physical health. Do not drive your business objectives forward in spite of your mental or physical health. All the financial achievement in the world cannot buy your health back once it is compromised badly enough. Invest in your health by scheduling time for exercise, eating sensibly, and listening to your body. By listening to your body, I also mean not ignoring the physical signs that tell you things are going off track. From shortness of breath to poor sleep, to weight gain or pains on moving. These are all the signs that you need to listen more closely to what your body is telling you. See your physician regularly and share these signs openly.

Pamper to rejuvenate yourself. Take time for you to be pampered. This can come in many ways — from booking a regular massage, to personal grooming, to that quiet time spent with a glass of wine or tea and a good book, and even cat napping. Whatever your idea of pampering is, it is up to you to do it. These mental getaways of indulgence can have amazing positive effects on your mind and body.

LIST THREE **PERSONAL** LIFE TIME GOALS YOU WOULD
LIKE TO ACHIEVE AND WHEN YOU WILL ACHIEVE THEM

LIST THREE GOALS TO ACHIEVE IN THE NEXT YEAR
(LIST THE DATE YOU WILL ACHIEVE THEM)

LIST THREE GOALS TO ACHIEVE IN THE NEXT THREE YEARS
(LIST THE DATE YOU WILL ACHIEVE THEM)

SECRET TIP 10

" build

your

SROI

"

———•———

That is, build a social return on investment. Connecting your business directly to the support of a charitable cause will require you to review the upside potential for any pursuit. In a capitalist market economy, business exists to produce profit for the goods and/or services it provides in order to reinvest and grow the business as well as pay its shareholders. That is the definition of a for-profit business. In the non-profit world, the so-called profit is redirected to social good and/or their designated beneficiaries and by the direct tangible benefit to the cause. As well, it is consumed by supporting, promoting, or helping administer the organization. The evidence of a return in non-profit work is sometimes hard to find on first glance and sometimes even harder to measure when dealing with social impact. It will take effort to determine just what success looks like and how it will be measured. Sponsors or donors expect no financial return other than the intrinsic rewards of giving, the affiliation with the cause, and the tax credit that might come for the gift or advertising expense. Although I believe they really should, most donors rarely even hold the organization accountable to measuring or reporting some form of SROI.

As an entrepreneur deploying a charitable giving or social enterprise strategy,

it will be very important for you to be able to measure your SROI to learn whether you are making an impact

or whether the initiative is worth continuing. While a goal would be to create a sustainable financial model to allow for the enterprise to continue, it will be likely that this entity will require fundraising on an ongoing basis. This will be derived from you, your business, and possibly other external donors or stakeholders of the enterprise. Economics professionals would argue that you can pretty much quantify anything, and thus measure the success or effectiveness of it. I agree. In fact, economics can even guide or change behaviors. You will need to be fairly astute to truly understand the economic impact of your efforts. Take for instance the challenge of homelessness and you were to develop a social enterprise that funds building affordable homes. What would the economic impact be for a family that might move in? Well, for starters, with a permanent address, they could be more employable, thus earn more and pay more taxes. They might make lifetime income of a million dollars, paying three hundred thousand in taxes and investing in local businesses by consuming in their community. Their children would be more secure and comfortable and likely be able to focus more in school, thus improving their opportunity for success or employment in their adulthood. The residual effect of this stability could also be that they interrupt a pattern of poverty and raise their own productive family. The list goes on. These are measurable economic benefits. Other benefits will be the reduction of social, health and economic costs. However, if you were not successful, in sheltering just one family, you will affect even more taxpayers; placing a burden on our social, health and maybe even justice systems. SROI is very much measurable; you simply have to identify the meaningful data — either in the positive impact, or the societal costs.

How you engage in implementing a charitable strategy that results in a positive SROI, will fall back on what your strengths are — personally, and as a business. It seems natural for a company in the homebuilding business to engage in a homeless initiative. Same goes for a grocery chain to actively be involved with the local food bank. But what does your energy company do? In some ways, the sky is the limit...in others it might be more natural to engage in environmental pursuits. You can direct money, time, or influence to a cause. The choice is yours.

WHAT IS/ARE YOUR CHARITABLE CAUSE(S)?

WHAT ARE THE OBJECTIVE MEASUREMENTS
YOU CAN MAKE FOR SUCCESSFUL IMPACT?

WHAT ARE THE OBJECTIVE MEASUREMENTS OR IMPACTS
THAT RESULT FROM YOU DOING NOTHING?

GIVE back

SECRET TIP 11

" give

for

happiness

"

———————

It truly is better to do so than to receive. Study after study has shown that the

happiness derived from giving has a significant measurable emotional and physical benefit for the giver.

A study done by Great Britain researchers, published in the *Journal of Social Psychology,* looked at acts of kindness. In a ten day experiment, they formed three groups; one to perform a daily act of kindness, the other to do something new each day, and the last had no instructions. In the follow up satisfaction survey, the subjective measurement of happiness was the greatest in the group who had performed random acts of kindness. Researchers at Harvard Business School and the University of British Columbia published their findings online in the *Journal of Happiness Studies.* Beforehand, they had given their participants sums of money and asked that they choose to either spend it on themselves or on someone else in such a manner that made them happiest. They had already provided their recollection of what both acts felt like to them from their past. At the conclusion of the study results were reviewed. The first important discovery was the fact that the strongest happiness memories were following giving to someone else. The next very interesting finding was that those who recalled happiness from giving in the past were most likely to give in the present (future). This implies somewhat of a feedback loop of giving and happiness. Anecdotally we've heard that what we give comes back to us. This study confirms this statement and suggests we actually feed off this energy.

Further evidence of the giving effect on happiness was found by researchers (Aknin, L., Barrington-Leigh, C., Dunn, E., Helliwell, J.,

Burns, J., Biswas-Diener, R., Norton, M.) published in 2013 in the *Journal of Personality* and *Social Psychology* (page 635-652). Here are their comments from their study named *Prosocial Spending and Well-Being: Cross-cultural Evidence for a Psychological Universal*:

> "*Human beings around the world derive emotional benefits from using their financial resources to help others*" (prosocial spending).

> "*Prosocial spending is associated with greater happiness around the world, in poor and rich countries alike.*"

> "*Our findings suggest that the reward experienced from helping others may be deeply ingrained in human nature, emerging in diverse cultural and economic contexts.*"

While two parties benefit in the act of giving, there can be a disproportionately larger benefit to the giver than the recipient of charity. There are chemical effects that occur as endorphins are released that provide a bit of a high when we perform the pleasurable act of goodness. Our brains are very well tuned to reward us when our pleasure centers are affected. As well, there are social benefits to philanthropy as those who give can consider themselves as contributors (versus takers) within society. Lastly, there are also financial benefits from giving. From tax benefits, to access to events and activities, and direct recognition, there are all sorts of financial benefits available to donors.

Establishing an ongoing or long term giving strategy for you and your business will allow you to experience that happiness repeatedly. Additionally, you are making available the gift of giving to your customers and stakeholders too. If given the choice of buying services or products from companies which support charity versus those which do not, consumers will support those who do give. In fact, a Forbes article from December 15, 2010 showed that 83 percent of consumers polled believed that companies should support charities and non-profits, and as such consumers would be more inclined to buy from those companies. Wouldn't you want your customers to be happier as a result of their support of your company over others?

RECALL A TIME WHEN YOU GAVE

AND HOW IT MADE YOU FEEL

PERFORM RANDOM ACTS OF KINDNESS FOR THE NEXT

FIVE DAYS AND RECORD YOUR ACTS HERE:

- ❧ RANDOM ACT OF KINDNESS DAY ONE:

- ❧ RANDOM ACT OF KINDNESS DAY TWO:

- ❧ RANDOM ACT OF KINDNESS DAY THREE:

- ❧ RANDOM ACT OF KINDNESS DAY FOUR:

- ❧ RANDOM ACT OF KINDNESS DAY FIVE:

SECRET TIP 12

" give

your

time

"

You can do this on your own, you can encourage your employees to do this, and you can challenge your peers to volunteer their time. Consider offering one day per month (or per quarter) to your employees to spend serving charity — on a paid basis. This is a major thing your business can do to help charity directly and it will build increased loyalty for your employees. In fact, as a twist, canvas your employees for the top five charities they would like to support and then place them in a rotation for the year.

When you choose to give time personally, you should reflect again on your strengths, and then make decisions such as joining advisory boards or Board of Directors' roles. You could take on a committee lead role, or lead an event or campaign. While volunteering your time is as valuable as any funding could ever be, your participation in this capacity will likely give you a greater sense of pride and understanding of what exactly the charity faces in terms of challenges and opportunities. This knowledge can improve the effectiveness of your future philanthropy.

Giving time returns valuable experience to you.

In one simple act of volunteerism, you gain knowledge of the cause, you learn about people you might not have ever met, you gain a perspective that will likely be from the beneficiaries point of view, and you might even gain a new understanding of the challenges faced by leaders who are trying to make an impact.

I have volunteered in so many ways over the years, that I have lost track of all the time I've committed. From organizational and event committees, to Board of Directors and roundtables, to sorting food at the local Food Bank, and serving meals to the homeless, I have done a lot. The one thing I have been doing for the past eight consecutive years is my role as a volunteer coach of my daughter's soccer teams. A three or four evening per week commitment for all those years is quite an investment. I believe I have been able to give back to the young girls on the various teams in ways that I might never fully understand. For some it is simply the coaching, for others it has been the discipline, some might have been able to achieve more than they ever expected with the guidance and support provided, and others simply needed a father figure in their lives. Whatever the impact, it has been a tremendously rewarding experience.

Committing your time in such a significant way might not appeal to you. Your schedule might not be conducive to it. However, if you can volunteer your time in an impactful way with whatever cause that resonates most with you, you will find incredible rewards in the effort.

WHERE WILL YOU GIVE YOUR TIME?

COMMIT TO A CONTINUOUS SCHEDULE
OF VOLUNTEERING RIGHT NOW.
WHAT TIME IN YOUR WEEK
WILL YOU DEVOTE TO VOLUNTEERING?

SECRET TIP 13

> " give
>
>   money "

While sometimes you might not think so, you have plenty of resources to choose from. These assets include human capital, business profits, personal funds, employee funds, supplier funds, customer support, etc. There are also goods and services that you might contribute. All should be considered when deciding to make a financial gift. There are many strategies to give. Some will be simply reflected as a line item or expenses or tax credits, others might be infrastructure investment or marketing funds. Entertainment or event fundraising is also possible. Here are a few practical considerations and strategies you can use to give:

Corporate

Giving through financial sponsorship, profit sharing (donating a fixed percentage of profits), or funding infrastructure development for a cause or charity can be ways for your company to give. Think of funding the purchase of computer systems and hardware for a charity. This links your business directly to the effort and provides a strong community message. It is also an effective way to provide funds directly to a charity and most likely will offer a useable taxable expense for your annual filings.

Engaging employees and customers can be done as well. You might organize your own customer appreciation event with all proceeds going to a single charity or multiple charities. You might even promote contests or challenges that encourage customer buying or promotional activities by offering to match or donate a portion of their purchases. You could even reward them with a donation in their name and recognize them for simply being a customer or renewing or upgrading a purchase. Years ago, when I was more actively transacting securities in my financial investment business, I launched a birthday "thank you" promotion, where I would donate to my charitable fund $5 per transaction for every transaction made by my clients in their birthday month. I sent a simple birthday card that had the statement *"Giving back to the community — in your honour"*, sent a birthday wish and provided a personal note with their "donation amount" as well as details of the promotion. It was something our clients appreciated very much.

When thinking about pooling charitable funds from events, promotions, etc., for your corporate giving, you might even wish to consider establishing a formal foundation which will manage the charitable giving aspects and reporting. Your company would collect the funds allocated to charity, then plainly make a single regular donation to the foundation and receive its tax receipts, while the foundation would be responsible for the disbursements. This also streamlines giving such as profit sharing by directing a percentage of profits to the foundation monthly or quarterly, and then granting to multiple charities or causes throughout each year. There would not be a hurried decision needed each time profits are realized, as to which charities will receive them. The giving strategy can be constructed more methodically within the foundation's framework. This can be a very public way for your company to express your philanthropy, while simultaneously supporting causes that matter to you and your company and providing customers a means to further identify with you at a personal level. Lastly, there is a simple tax credit earned for the corporation at the time when the gift is made. Thus a foundation also adds to the tax planning options for your business.

Personal

My goal is to help entrepreneurs make more money and thus increase their capacity to give. In fact, I hope to coach entrepreneurs to help them make a billion dollars in revenue that will allow them to re-direct $100 million in profits to charity over the next ten years. I encourage giving through your business on an ongoing basis, but also looking at your personal situation to investigate where giving fits in your life. Will you give now, or give later? Or both? What will you give? There are many ways to give. Everything from gifts of cash or securities, to assigning charity as the beneficiary of an insurance policy, setting up a private foundation or Donor Advised Fund. Most importantly, sophisticated financial planning is required.

We are motivated to give because it is important to us and we have a sense of responsibility and altruism. It is true there are great ways to do this and then there are poor ways. You work extraordinarily hard for your money. You have taken risks and you do your due diligence when taking on new initiatives.

Do not allow anything less than that care when planning your giving.

Determine how you will give the most to impact the best possible outcome for the charities or causes your support. Planning can be a powerful tool when contemplating your philanthropic giving. It will increase the effectiveness of your gifts. It will also help you ensure succession of your family wealth.

Using philanthropic giving incorporated into your personal or corporate tax planning and the succession of your wealth will uncover ways to give much more than you ever thought possible, while reducing or removing the impact of income

&/or estate taxation. We teach entrepreneurs and baby boomers how they can plan for a zero tax estate, while passing their estate intact to their heirs. It is never too early to begin planning to take control of your philanthropy. Seek an expert to help you with these decisions.

WILL YOU GIVE CORPORATELY?

DO YOU HOPE TO GIVE PERSONALLY AS WELL?

▶ WHAT DO YOU GIVE TO CHARITY EACH YEAR?

▶ WHAT STRATEGIES DO YOU USE TO GIVE NOW?

▶ WHAT STRATEGIES WOULD YOU LIKE TO INVESTIGATE
   FURTHER?

SECRET TIP 14

" give

influence "

When you are a leader in business and your community, you are capable of influencing people and their behavior.

When you direct attention to important causes or activities you are able to create big impact.

You should be clear about the causes that are important to you and your customers. Use your platform to raise awareness.

Engage your peers and networks in the charitable activities you do and the events you hold. While your focus might be on your business, by connecting your actions to a philanthropic goal you influence others to be moved to act. This does not require you to volunteer, or even give money, it is something more intangible.

I have spoken about Oprah Winfrey on more than one occasion. Her biggest contribution to charity has been her understanding of the position she is in. The "Oprah effect" is all about influence. People focus on the incredible monetary gifts and the millions raised for various causes and charities when they think about Oprah's charity. In fact, she has done more for literacy than almost anyone in America. Oprah changed the way people approached reading and turned authors into heroes — and millionaires. Her Angel Network, established in 1997, has raised millions for charity, funded scholarships, and built homes. None of this happened by accident, Oprah always understood that one of her biggest assets was the media platform from which she had incredible reach. Influence is what she has leveraged to make a huge impact in this world.

WHERE MIGHT YOU HAVE AN INFLUENCE
OVER A GROUP OF PEOPLE?
WHERE CAN YOU REACH A BROAD AUDIENCE DIRECTLY?

HOW CAN YOU DELIVER A MESSAGE OF GIVING
TO THEM?

HOW CAN YOU INSPIRE PARTICIPATION IN GIVING?

SECRET TIP 15

"
give

now
"

What a concept! Seems simple and it is. Do not over think this! As you know, smart and successful entrepreneurs make decisions fast. As I have stated, they set criteria, check the boxes in their minds and act decisively.

There is no reason to delay your philanthropy. Give back now and plan to give more in the future.

Start something important and get it moving right away.

Naturally you will want to plan things through to ensure you will have a big impact. Let's review the upside of giving. The first big impact is that someone or something benefits from your philanthropy. Next, YOU are able to make that impact and build your legacy. The third, you get to experience more happiness. Lastly, you can use charitable giving to reduce or even eradicate one of the biggest threats to your wealth — TAXES. Estate taxes will steal from your heirs and reallocate your financial resources to the bureaucracy of government. You must take control of your money and your legacy and re-direct your "social" capital towards the causes and institutions that are most important to you and your family. As you do this, you will effectively reduce your taxes. There are intelligent financial planning tools that you can use — especially at a younger age (under 55 years old) — such as insurance. In fact, insurance combined with charitable giving can even help you achieve a zero tax estate if the approach is right for you. Seek the assistance of a qualified expert to help develop the plan and identify the right strategies and tactics for your family.

One other threat to your wealth is a bigger concern than even taxes. The taxman will threaten your wealth and your heirs' inheritance, but health problems will threaten your life and steal your impact. While you are still healthy you must act. Plan to give and do it now, or at least set your giving in motion. You might know the old Chinese proverb asking when a good time to plant a tree is. Of course it is decades ago, but when is the next best time to plant a tree? Today.

Here's a short comment about implementing philanthropy and using professionals to help you do this. Generally speaking, your financial and/or investment advisors won't necessarily educate you on this topic. Charitable giving threatens them. They are fearful they will lose assets (they usually are compensated on the assets they manage) and there is a perceived lack of compensation connected to charitable giving. They are also concerned you will re-direct your attention from their agenda — which should be, but might not always be consistent with yours. Finally, and most likely, they often lack knowledge in the area of legacy giving. Planned giving is not a widely understood area of knowledge in the investment community.

A lot of advisors don't even want to have the important yet uncomfortable conversation about mortality with their clients. They are either afraid to ask and are uncomfortable with the topic. They might even be afraid you might actually want to engage them in a deeper conversation and that they are not equipped to handle things. Finally, and not to be dismissed, is the fact they just do not really care to get involved with this side of your financial life.

While making a decision to act on your philanthropic intent might be a simple step, finding the expert to guide you through this journey could be slightly more challenging. Don't be dismayed, there are plenty of credible and knowledgeable specialists who can help you. It is important that you do your homework to find them.

WHAT STEPS WILL YOU TAKE TODAY
TO EXECUTE YOUR BIG IMPACT GIVING?

DO YOU HAVE THE RIGHT SPECIALISTS IN YOUR LIFE
TO HELP YOU WITH THIS? LIST THEM:

▶ LAWYER:

▶ FINANCIAL PLANNER OR ADVISOR:

▶ ACCOUNTANT:

▶ INSURANCE AGENT:

▶ OTHER TRUSTED ADVISORS:

SECRET TIP 16

" *give later*

to leave your legacy "

Commit to give back for the community, for you, and for your legacy. This is the planning part. We talked about giving now. Well, it takes planning now to give big in the future. When I meet with any family who wishes to plan their estate succession and legacy giving we ask them to imagine their own Norman Rockwell painting of their future. This will be their vision of what they want for themselves, how much they hope to pass on to their heirs, and then the impact they would like to achieve through charitable giving. You have to work to envision your ideal outcome because most people will view their own future through current lenses. In order to put people in the right frame of mind, I encourage them to

view their legacy through their grandchildrens' eyes.

Proper planning starts with the right strategic financial advisor. You know you have the right expert if they begin by listening to you and guiding you through a values discussion that helps them understand YOUR vision of the future. A strategic advisor will help you determine the goals for your four "P's". Personal, provide, protect, and preserve. They will build goals for the four "P's" based on your vision and values. "Personal" goals most directly reflect your values. They can include the things you hope to do, experience, buy, give, etc. Travel and lifestyle, volunteering, giving back, health, and creative pursuits are most often reflected here. "Provide" covers income and funding your current and future lifestyle.

Goals will identify how your assets will provide the cash flow you need to pay for the necessities and the things you hope to do. "Protect" to insulate you and your wealth against the five biggest threats to your wealth. They include health, litigation, creditors, marriage dissolution, and taxes. Quantifying what these will or can cost you as well as identifying the structures and tools you can best use to insulate you and your family from the threats will be discussed. When taxes come into the picture, succession and legacy soon follow. "Preserve" is all about preserving your wealth in succession. This will involve planning to pass on your wealth to heirs while reducing taxes in the process. We have been able to plan zero tax estates for people. Philanthropic giving makes this possible. There are three decisions to make when considering your succession goals. 1) Do nothing, pay your "fair share" of taxes and pass on whatever's left to your heirs, 2) Give charitably to re-direct your tax dollars away from the government, to causes that are important to you and pass on the rest to your heirs, or 3) Use tools, such as insurance and planned giving strategies to give charitably, cut out the tax man completely and pass on all your wealth, intact, to your heirs.

Number three is the preferred strategy of the wealthiest families in North America. Insurance delivers the succession outcomes for your goals by replacing estate assets. In fact adding charity as the named beneficiaries of your life insurance will allow you to earn tax credits that could match your estate tax obligations, allowing you to pass on your wealth in its entirety.

What are your "personal" goals?

▸ Have you considered and written down your personal goals?

What are your "provide" goals?

▸ Are you comfortable that your required lifestyle income needs will be covered?

Do you have the right specialists in your life to help you with this? List them:

▸ Do you understand the five threats to your wealth and have you considered protecting against or preparing for them?

Do you have the right specialists in your life to help you with this? List them:

▸ Have you considered what you wish to leave in succession for your family (and friends)?

▸ Do you have a bigger plan to leave assets to charity?

▸ What would be your ideal outcome in legacy planning?

SECRET TIP 17

" *reflect* "

Part of giving back is reflecting on the things in your life that you have experienced, acquired, invented, or built. Instead of always charging forward,

take a moment to reflect on the good you do and have done.

It is important to appreciate your contribution.

It will energize you and refocus you on your purposeful life.

Use the opportunity to learn from your successes and missteps.

Taking a moment to reflect demands that we free up time as well as mental and emotional space to contemplate our lives and everything around us. Reflection is the first step toward gratitude and it is vital, yet when I work with successful businessmen and women, whether they're entrepreneurs, professionals or senior executives with high-profile firms, I've noticed they invariably focus on what's next. They are so driven, they rarely take the time to look at what they've accomplished today, let alone what they have achieved last month, last year, or five years prior.

While I do appreciate and applaud their commitment to looking ahead as they plan, push, and inspire themselves and those around them to do more and do it better, I rarely see them pause to truly reflect on their results or really celebrate their victories.

Looking back is important in business but also in life and in philanthropy. It allows us to recognize the results of our efforts and actions in order to further develop the experience, expertise, and confidence required to maintain the momentum and focus on new targets.

RECALL AND DESCRIBE THE MOST IMPORTANT
ACT OF GIVING YOU HAVE BEEN CONNECTED WITH

WHAT DID YOU LEARN FROM THE EXPERIENCE?

SECRET TIP 18

" express gratitude "

*"Piglet noticed that even though he had a Very Small Heart,
it could hold a rather large amount of Gratitude."*

— A.A. Milne, *Winnie-the-Pooh*

Gratitude allows us to be thankful for the experiences we have had

— good or bad. Sharing that gratitude with others is also important. When good things happen with any endeavor you must acknowledge them to yourself and then share those successes with your colleagues, family, and friends. Openly being grateful and expressing gratitude can be challenging, and I think business leaders find it extremely challenging as well. But it is absolutely critical. What makes gratitude so special is how it feels to receive the true gratitude of someone who expresses it from their very inner core.

5 things to do every day to show gratitude

1. **Say thank you** — this small phrase packs a ton of meaning. A simple thank you to anyone who has offered of themselves in any way to you deserves this much. You deserve to share your appreciation for them.

2. **Thank your family** — every day you must share with your family (parents, spouse, children, grandparents, etc.) just how much they matter to your life. Thank them for their unconditional love and share yours.

3. **Acknowledge those who help** — making a point of

showing your gratitude for the work of someone is important for them individually, but sharing your appreciation with others about that person is a compliment of gratitude that will lift them up in the eyes and minds of others.

4. **Focus on the joys of what you have accomplished** — remind yourself daily of the things you have done to get where you are. Be grateful that you have accomplished a life of experiences that have shaped who you are. The things you view as minor or simply a part of your life could be considered tremendous accomplishments. Give yourself the gratitude of a job well done.

5. **Be grateful for the challenges that lie ahead** — embracing life's challenges and not shying away from them emboldens you to succeed. Opportunities on the horizon help you grow, learn, and expand the fullness of your life.

Acknowledgements

So many people have shared so much with me over the years. Their input, wisdom, guidance and mentorship have impacted my life in so many ways. There have been so many of you, it is difficult to thank everyone, and I apologize if I did not mention. I am eternally grateful for you all.

As I reflect on all your influences, I share my thanks with my family, Sherri, Madison, Coen and my parents, Don and Maureen, first and foremost. Thank you to: Keith Thompson, James Malinchak, Scott Keffer, Dr. Danny Brassell, Kevin Clayson, John Formica, Barry Spencer, Marylin Suey, Dan S. Kennedy, Dianna Campbell-Smith, Howard Schultz, Michael LePage, Glen Coskey, Karl Vanderleest, Kelly and Mary Aldridge, Dan Holinda, Michael Permack, W. Brett Wilson, Chris Hamilton, John Leishman, Keith Macphail, Alvin Libin, T. Harv Eker, Craig and Marc Kielburger, Malala Yousafzai, Magic Johnson, Danielle Decceco, Tasso Chondronikolis, Daren Shaw, Sam Switzer, Richard Branson, Dave "aka Famous Dave" Anderson, Christine Salberg, Allan Markin, Darcy Hulston, Dan Sullivan, Brianne Graham, Jeff Polovik, Jeffrey Grubert, Penny Walker, Terri Hardin Jackson, Din Ladak, Robert Jordan, Brian Tracey, Seth Godin, Blake Mycoskie, Andre Agassi, Kevin Eastman, Kathy Kolbe, Birgitte & Colin (in Memory of) Michie, Oprah Winfrey, Paul Alofs, Nikola Elkins.

Help others GROW, GET and GIVE!
Share this book!

Retail: $19.95

Special Quantity Discounts

5 – 20 books	$17.95
21 – 50 books	$15.95
100 – 499 books	$14.95
500 + books	$10.95

To place an order, contact:

(403) 870-6775

info@mikeskrypnek.com

www.mikeskrypnek.com

www.BigGROWTHBigIMPACTSummit.com

Made in the USA
Charleston, SC
11 November 2014